THE

INTEREST OF AMERICA

IN

SEA POWER,

PRESENT AND FUTURE.

BY

CAPTAIN A. T. MAHAN, D.C.L., LL.D.
United States Navy.

KENNIKAT PRESS
Port Washington, N. Y./London

KENNIKAT PRESS SCHOLARLY REPRINTS

Dr. Ralph Adams Brown, Senior Editor

Series on
MAN AND HIS ENVIRONMENT
Under the General Editorial Supervision of
Dr. Roger C. Heppell
Professor of Geography, State University of New York

THE INTEREST OF AMERICA IN
SEA POWER, PRESENT AND FUTURE

First published in 1897
Reissued in 1970 by Kennikat Press
Library of Congress Catalog Card No: 70-113290
ISBN 0-8046-1325-7

Manufactured by Taylor Publishing Company   Dallas, Texas

KENNIKAT SERIES ON MAN AND HIS ENVIRONMENT

PREFACE.

———◆———

WHATEVER interest may be possessed by a collection of detached papers, issued at considerable intervals during a term of several years, and written without special reference one to the other, or, at the first, with any view to subsequent publication, depends as much upon the date at which they were composed, and the condition of affairs then existent, as it does upon essential unity of treatment. If such unity perchance be found in these, it will not be due to antecedent purpose, but to the fact that they embody the thought of an individual mind, consecutive in the line of its main conceptions, but adjusting itself continually to changing conditions, which the progress of events entails.

The author, therefore, has not sought to bring these papers down to the present date;

to reconcile seeming contradictions, if such there be; to suppress repetitions; or to weld into a consistent whole the several parts which in their origin were independent. Such changes as have been made extend only to phraseology, with the occasional modification of an expression that seemed to err by excess or defect. The dates at the head of each article show the time of its writing, not of its publication.

The thanks of the author are expressed to the proprietors of the " Atlantic Monthly," of the " Forum," of the " North American Review," and of " Harper's New Monthly Magazine," who have kindly permitted the republication of the articles originally contributed to their pages.

A. T. MAHAN.

November, 1897.

CONTENTS.

MAPS.

THE UNITED STATES LOOKING OUTWARD.

THE UNITED STATES LOOKING OUTWARD.

August, 1890.

INDICATIONS are not wanting of an approaching change in the thoughts and policy of Americans as to their relations with the world outside their own borders. For the past quarter of a century, the predominant idea, which has asserted itself successfully at the polls and shaped the course of the government, has been to preserve the home market for the home industries. The employer and the workman alike have been taught to look at the various economical measures proposed from this point of view, to regard with hostility any step favoring the intrusion of the foreign producer upon their own domain, and rather to demand increasingly rigorous measures of exclusion than to acquiesce in any loosening of the chain that binds the consumer to them.

The inevitable consequence has followed, as in all cases when the mind or the eye is exclusively fixed in one direction, that the danger of loss or the prospect of advantage in another quarter has been overlooked; and although the abounding resources of the country have maintained the exports at a high figure, this flattering result has been due more to the superabundant bounty of Nature than to the demand of other nations for our protected manufactures.

For nearly the lifetime of a generation, therefore, American industries have been thus protected, until the practice has assumed the force of a tradition, and is clothed in the mail of conservatism.   In their mutual relations, these industries resemble the activities of a modern ironclad that has heavy armor, but inferior engines and guns; mighty for defence, weak for offence.   Within, the home market is secured; but outside, beyond the broad seas, there are the markets of the world, that can be entered and controlled only by a vigorous contest, to which the habit of trusting to protection by statute does not conduce.

At bottom, however, the temperament of the American people is essentially alien to such a sluggish attitude. Independently of all bias for or against protection, it is safe to predict that, when the opportunities for gain abroad are understood, the course of American enterprise will cleave a channel by which to reach them. Viewed broadly, it is a most welcome as well as significant fact that a prominent and influential advocate of protection, a leader of the party committed to its support, a keen reader of the signs of the times and of the drift of opinion, has identified himself with a line of policy which looks to nothing less than such modifications of the tariff as may expand the commerce of the United States to all quarters of the globe. Men of all parties can unite on the words of Mr. Blaine, as reported in a recent speech : " It is not an ambitious destiny for so great a country as ours to manufacture only what we can consume, or produce only what we can eat." In face of this utterance of so shrewd and able a public man, even the extreme character of the recent tariff legislation seems but a sign of the coming change, and brings to mind that famous Continental System, of which our own is the analogue, to support which Napoleon added legion to legion and enterprise to enterprise, till the fabric of the Empire itself crashed beneath the weight.

The interesting and significant feature of this changing attitude is the turning of the eyes outward, instead of inward only, to seek the welfare of the country. To affirm the importance of distant markets, and the relation to them of our own immense powers of production, implies logically the recognition of the link that joins the products and the markets, — that is, the carrying trade; the three together constituting that chain of maritime power to which Great Britain owes her wealth and greatness. Further, is it too much to say that, as two of these links, the shipping and the markets, are exterior to our own borders, the acknowledgment of them carries with it a view of the relations of the United States to the world radically distinct from the simple idea of self-sufficingness? We shall not follow far this line of thought before there will dawn the realization of America's unique position, facing the older worlds of the East and West, her shores washed by the oceans which touch the one or the other, but which are common to her alone.

Coincident with these signs of change in our own policy there is a restlessness in the world at large which is deeply significant, if not ominous. It is beside our purpose to dwell upon the internal state of Europe, whence, if disturbances arise, the effect upon us may be but partial and indirect. But the great seaboard powers there do not stand on guard against their continental rivals only; they cherish also aspirations for commercial extension, for colonies, and for influence in distant regions, which may bring, and, even under our present contracted policy, already have brought them into collision with ourselves. The incident of the Samoa Islands, trivial apparently, was nevertheless eminently suggestive of European ambitions. America then roused from sleep as to interests closely concerning her future. At this moment internal troubles are imminent in the Sandwich Islands, where it should be our fixed determination to allow no foreign influence to equal our own. All over the world German commercial and colonial push is coming into collision with other nations: witness the affair of the Caroline Islands with Spain; the partition of New Guinea with England;

the yet more recent negotiation between these
two powers concerning their share in Africa,
viewed with deep distrust and jealousy by
France; the Samoa affair; the conflict between
German control and American interests in the
islands of the western Pacific; and the alleged
progress of German influence in Central and
South America. It is noteworthy that, while
these various contentions are sustained with
the aggressive military spirit characteristic of
the German Empire, they are credibly said to
arise from the national temper more than from
the deliberate policy of the government, which
in this matter does not lead, but follows, the
feeling of the people, — a condition much more
formidable.

There is no sound reason for believing that
the world has passed into a period of assured
peace outside the limits of Europe. Unsettled
political conditions, such as exist in Haïti,
Central America, and many of the Pacific
islands, especially the Hawaiian group, when
combined with great military or commercial
importance as is the case with most of these
positions, involve, now as always, dangerous
germs of quarrel, against which it is prudent at

least to be prepared. Undoubtedly, the general temper of nations is more averse from war than it was of old. If no less selfish and grasping than our predecessors, we feel more dislike to the discomforts and sufferings attendant upon a breach of peace; but to retain that highly valued repose and the undisturbed enjoyment of the returns of commerce, it is necessary to argue upon somewhat equal terms of strength with an adversary. It is the preparedness of the enemy, and not acquiescence in the existing state of things, that now holds back the armies of Europe.

On the other hand, neither the sanctions of international law nor the justice of a cause can be depended upon for a fair settlement of differences, when they come into conflict with a strong political necessity on the one side opposed to comparative weakness on the other. In our still-pending dispute over the seal-fishing of Bering Sea, whatever may be thought of the strength of our argument, in view of generally admitted principles of international law, it is beyond doubt that our contention is reasonable, just, and in the interest of the world at large. But in the attempt to enforce it we have come into collision not only with national susceptibilities as to the honor of the flag, which we ourselves very strongly share, but also with a state governed by a powerful necessity, and exceedingly strong where we are particularly weak and exposed. Not only has Great Britain a mighty navy and we a long defenceless seacoast, but it is a great commercial and political advantage to her that her larger colonies, and above all Canada, should feel that the power of the mother country is something which they need, and upon which they can count. The dispute is between the United States and Canada, not the United States and Great Britain; but it has been ably used by the latter to promote the solidarity of sympathy between herself and her colony. With the mother country alone an equitable arrangement, conducive to well-understood mutual interests, could be reached readily; but the purely local and peculiarly selfish wishes of Canadian fishermen dictate the policy of Great Britain, because Canada is the most important link uniting her to her colonies and maritime interests in the Pacific. In case of a European war, it is possible that the British navy will not be able to hold open the route through the Mediterranean to the East; but having a strong naval station at Halifax, and another at Esquimalt, on the Pacific, the two connected by the Canadian Pacific Railroad, England possesses an alternate line of communication far less exposed to maritime aggression than the former, or than the third route by the Cape of Good Hope, as well as two bases essential to the service of her commerce, or other naval operations, in the North Atlantic and the Pacific. Whatever arrangement of this question is finally reached, the fruit of Lord Salisbury's attitude scarcely can fail to be a strengthening of the sentiments of attachment to, and reliance upon, the mother country, not only in Canada, but in the other great colonies. These feelings of attachment and mutual dependence supply the living spirit, without which the nascent schemes for Imperial Federation are but dead mechanical contrivances; nor are they without influence upon such generally unsentimental considerations as those of buying and selling, and the course of trade.

This dispute, seemingly paltry yet really serious, sudden in its appearance and dependent for its issue upon other considerations than its own merits, may serve to convince us of many latent and yet unforeseen dangers to the peace of the western hemisphere, attendant upon the opening of a canal through the Central American Isthmus. In a general way, it is evident enough that this canal, by modifying the direction of trade routes, will induce a great increase of commercial activity and carrying trade throughout the Caribbean Sea; and that this now comparatively deserted nook of the ocean will become, like the Red Sea, a great thoroughfare of shipping, and will attract, as never before in our day, the interest and ambition of maritime nations. Every position in that sea will have enhanced commercial and military value, and the canal itself will become a strategic centre of the most vital importance. Like the Canadian Pacific Railroad, it will be a link between the two oceans; but, unlike it, the use, unless most carefully guarded by treaties, will belong wholly to the belligerent which controls the sea by its naval power. In case of war, the United States will unquestionably command the Canadian Railroad, despite the deterrent force of operations by the hostile navy upon our seaboard; but no less unquestionably will she be impotent, as against any of the great maritime powers, to control the Central American canal. Militarily speaking, and having reference to European complications only, the piercing of the Isthmus is nothing but a disaster to the United States, in the present state of her military and naval preparation. It is especially dangerous to the Pacific coast; but the increased exposure of one part of our seaboard reacts unfavorably upon the whole military situation.

Despite a certain great original superiority conferred by our geographical nearness and immense resources, — due, in other words, to our natural advantages, and not to our intelligent preparations, — the United States is wofully unready, not only in fact but in purpose, to assert in the Caribbean and Central America a weight of influence proportioned to the extent of her interests. We have not the navy, and, what is worse, we are not willing to have the navy, that will weigh seriously in any disputes with those nations whose interests will conflict there with our own. We have not, and we are not anxious to provide, the defence of the seaboard which will leave the navy free for its work at sea. We have not, but many other powers have, positions, either within or on the borders of the Caribbean, which not only possess great natural advantages for the control of that sea, but have received and are receiving that artificial strength of fortification and armament which will make them practically inexpugnable. On the contrary, we have not on the Gulf of Mexico even the beginning of a navy yar which could serve as the base of our operations. Let me not be misunderstood. I am not regretting that we have not the means to meet on terms of equality the great navies of the Old World. I recognize, what few at least say, that, despite its great surplus revenue, this country is poor in proportion to its length of seaboard and its exposed points. That which I deplore, and which is a sober, just, and reasonable cause of deep national concern, is that the nation neither has nor cares to have its sea frontier so defended, and its navy of such power, as shall suffice, with the advantages of our position, to weigh seriously when inevitable discussions arise, — such as we have recently had about Samoa and Bering Sea, and which may at any moment come up about the Caribbean Sea or the canal. Is the United States, for instance, prepared to allow Germany to acquire the Dutch stronghold of Curaçao, fronting the Atlantic outlet of both the proposed canals of Panama and Nicaragua? Is she prepared to acquiesce in any foreign power purchasing from Haïti a naval station on the Windward Passage, through which pass our steamer routes to the Isthmus? Would she acquiesce in a foreign protectorate over the Sandwich Islands, that great central station of the Pacific, equidistant from San Francisco, Samoa, and the Marquesas, and an important post on our lines of communication with both Australia and China? Or will it be maintained that any one of these questions, supposing it to arise, is so exclusively one-sided, the arguments of policy and right so exclusively with us, that the other party will at once yield his eager wish, and gracefully withdraw? Was it so at Samoa? Is it so as regards

Bering Sea? The motto seen on so many ancient cannon, *Ultima ratio regum*, is not without its message to republics.

It is perfectly reasonable and legitimate, in estimating our needs of military preparation, to take into account the remoteness of the chief naval and military nations from our shores, and the consequent difficulty of maintaining operations at such a distance. It is equally proper, in framing our policy, to consider the jealousies of the European family of states, and their consequent unwillingness to incur the enmity of a people so strong as ourselves; their dread of our revenge in the future, as well as their inability to detach more than a certain part of their forces to our shores without losing much of their own weight in the councils of Europe. In truth, a careful determination of the force that Great Britain or France could probably spare for operations against our coasts, if the latter were suitably defended, without weakening their European position or unduly exposing their colonies and commerce, is the starting-point from which to calculate the strength of our own navy. If the latter be superior to the force that thus can be sent against it, and the coast be so defended as to leave the navy free to strike where it will, we can maintain our rights; not merely the rights which international law concedes, and which the moral sense of nations now supports, but also those equally real rights which, though not conferred by law, depend upon a clear preponderance of interest, upon obviously necessary policy, upon self-preservation, either total or partial. Were we so situated now in respect of military strength, we could secure our perfectly just claim as to the seal fisheries; not by seizing foreign ships on the open sea, but by the evident fact that, our cities being protected from maritime attack, our position and superior population lay open the Canadian Pacific, as well as the frontier of the Dominion, to do with as we please. Diplomats do not flourish such disagreeable truths in each other's faces; they look for a *modus vivendi*, and find it.

While, therefore, the advantages of our own position in the western hemisphere, and the disadvantages under which the operations of a European state would labor, are undeniable

2

and just elements in the calculations of the statesman, it is folly to look upon them as sufficient alone for our security. Much more needs to be cast into the scale that it may incline in favor of our strength. They are mere defensive factors, and partial at that. Though distant, our shores can be reached; being defenceless, they can detain but a short time a force sent against them. With a probability of three months' peace in Europe, no maritime power would fear to support its demands by a number of ships with which it would be loath indeed to part for a year.

Yet, were our sea frontier as strong as it now is weak, passive self-defence, whether in trade or war, would be but a poor policy, so long as this world continues to be one of struggle and vicissitude. All around us now is strife; " the struggle of life," " the race of life," are phrases so familiar that we do not feel their significance till we stop to think about them. Everywhere nation is arrayed against nation; our own no less than others. What is our protective system but an organized warfare? In carrying it on, it is true, we have only to use certain procedures which all states now concede to be a legal exercise of the national power, even though injurious to themselves. It is lawful, they say, to do what we will with our own. Are our people, however, so unaggressive that they are likely not to want their own way in matters where their interests turn on points of disputed right, or so little sensitive as to submit quietly to encroachment by others, in quarters where they long have considered their own influence should prevail?

Our self-imposed isolation in the matter of markets, and the decline of our shipping interest in the last thirty years, have coincided singularly with an actual remoteness of this continent from the life of the rest of the world. The writer has before him a map of the North and South Atlantic oceans, showing the direction of the principal trade routes and the proportion of tonnage passing over each; and it is curious to note what deserted regions, comparatively, are the Gulf of Mexico, the Caribbean Sea, and the adjoining countries and islands. A broad band stretches from our northern Atlantic coast to the English Channel; another as broad from the British Islands to the East, through the Mediterranean and Red Sea, over-flowing the borders of the latter in order to express the volume of trade. Around either cape — Good Hope and Horn — pass strips of about one-fourth this width, joining near the equator, midway between Africa and South America. From the West Indies issues a thread, indicating the present commerce of Great Britain with a region which once, in the Napoleonic wars, embraced one-fourth of the whole trade of the Empire. The significance is unmistakable: Europe has now little mer-cantile interest in the Caribbean Sea.

When the Isthmus is pierced, this isolation will pass away, and with it the indifference of foreign nations. From wheresoever they come and whithersoever they afterward go, all ships that use the canal will pass through the Carib-bean. Whatever the effect produced upon the prosperity of the adjacent continent and islands by the thousand wants attendant upon maritime activity, around such a focus of trade will centre large commercial and political interests. To protect and develop its own, each nation will seek points of support and means of influence in a quarter where the United States always has been jealously sensitive to the intrusion of European powers. The precise value of the Monroe doctrine is understood very loosely by most Americans, but the effect of the familiar phrase has been to develop a national sensitiveness, which is a more frequent cause of war than material interests; and over disputes caused by such feelings there will preside none of the calming influence due to the moral authority of international law, with its recognized principles, for the points in dispute will be of policy, of interest, not of conceded right. Already France and Great Britain are giving to ports held by them a degree of artificial strength uncalled for by their present importance. They look to the near future. Among the islands and on the mainland there are many positions of great importance, held now by weak or unstable states. Is the United States willing to see them sold to a powerful rival? But what right will she invoke against the transfer? She can allege but one, — that of her reasonable policy supported by her might.

Whether they will or no, Americans must now begin to look outward. The growing production of the country demands it. An increasing volume of public sentiment demands it. The position of the United States, between the two Old Worlds and the two great oceans, makes the same claim, which will soon be strengthened by the creation of the new link joining the Atlantic and Pacific. The tendency will be maintained and increased by the growth of the European colonies in the Pacific, by the advancing civilization of Japan, and by the rapid peopling of our Pacific States with men who have all the aggressive spirit of the advanced line of national progress. Nowhere does a vigorous foreign policy find more favor than among the people west of the Rocky Mountains.

It has been said that, in our present state of unpreparedness, a trans-isthmian canal will be a military disaster to the United States, and especially to the Pacific coast. When the canal is finished, the Atlantic seaboard will be neither more nor less exposed than it now is; it will merely share with the country at large the increased danger of foreign complications with inadequate means to meet them. The danger of the Pacific coast will be greater by so much as the way between it and Europe is shortened through a passage which the stronger maritime power can control. The danger will lie not merely in the greater facility for despatching a hostile squadron from Europe, but also in the fact that a more powerful fleet than formerly can be maintained on that coast by a European power, because it can be called home so much more promptly in case of need. The greatest weakness of the Pacific ports, however, if wisely met by our government, will go far to insure our naval superiority there. The two chief centres, San Francisco and Puget Sound, owing to the width and the great depth of the entrances, cannot be effectively protected by torpedoes; and consequently, as fleets can always pass batteries through an unobstructed channel, they cannot obtain perfect security by means of fortifications only. Valuable as such works will be to them, they must be further garrisoned by coast-defence ships, whose part in repelling an enemy will be co-ordinated with that of the batteries. The sphere of action of such ships should not be permitted to extend far beyond the port to which they are allotted, and of whose defence they form an essential part; but within that

sweep they will always be a powerful reinforce-
ment to the sea-going navy, when the strategic
conditions of a war cause hostilities to centre
around their port. By sacrificing power to go
long distances, the coast-defence ship gains proportionate weight of armor and guns; that is,
of defensive and offensive strength. It therefore adds an element of unique value to the
fleet with which it for a time acts. No foreign
states, except Great Britain, have ports so near
our Pacific coast as to bring it within the radius
of action of their coast-defence ships; and it is
very doubtful whether even Great Britain will
put such ships at Vancouver Island, the chief
value of which will be lost to her when the
Canadian Pacific is severed, — a blow always
in the power of this country. It is upon
our Atlantic seaboard that the mistress of
Halifax, of Bermuda, and of Jamaica will now
defend Vancouver and the Canadian Pacific.
In the present state of our seaboard defence
she can do so absolutely. What is all Canada
compared with our exposed great cities? Even
were the coast fortified, she still could do so,
if our navy be no stronger than is designed as
yet. What harm can we do Canada propor-

tionate to the injury we should suffer by the interruption of our coasting trade, and by a blockade of Boston, New York, the Delaware, and the Chesapeake? Such a blockade Great Britain certainly could make technically efficient, under the somewhat loose definitions of international law. Neutrals would accept it as such.

The military needs of the Pacific States, as well as their supreme importance to the whole country, are yet a matter of the future, but of a future so near that provision should begin immediately. To weigh their importance, consider what influence in the Pacific would be attributed to a nation comprising only the States of Washington, Oregon, and California, when filled with such men as now people them and still are pouring in, and which controlled such maritime centres as San Francisco, Puget Sound, and the Columbia River. Can it be counted less because they are bound by the ties of blood and close political union to the great communities of the East? But such influence, to work without jar and friction, requires underlying military readiness, like the proverbial iron hand under the velvet glove.

To provide this, three things are needful: First, protection of the chief harbors, by fortifications and coast-defence ships, which gives defensive strength, provides security to the community within, and supplies the bases necessary to all military operations. Secondly, naval force, the arm of offensive power, which alone enables a country to extend its influence outward. Thirdly, it should be an inviolable resolution of our national policy, that no foreign state should henceforth acquire a coaling position within three thousand miles of San Francisco, — a distance which includes the Hawaiian and Galapagos islands and the coast of Central America. For fuel is the life of modern naval war; it is the food of the ship; without it the modern monsters of the deep die of inanition. Around it, therefore, cluster some of the most important considerations of naval strategy. In the Caribbean and in the Atlantic we are confronted with many a foreign coal depot, bidding us stand to our arms, even as Carthage bade Rome; but let us not acquiesce in an addition to our dangers, a further diversion of our strength, by being forestalled in the North Pacific.

In conclusion, while Great Britain is undoubtedly the most formidable of our possible ene-
mies, both by her great navy and by the strong
positions she holds near our coasts, it must be
added that a cordial understanding with that
country is one of the first of our external interests. Both nations doubtless, and properly,
seek their own advantage; but both, also, are
controlled by a sense of law and justice, drawn
from the same sources, and deep-rooted in
their instincts. Whatever temporary aberra-
tion may occur, a return to mutual standards
of right will certainly follow. Formal alliance
between the two is out of the question, but a
cordial recognition of the similarity of character and ideas will give birth to sympathy,
which in turn will facilitate a co-operation ben-
eficial to both; for if sentimentality is weak,
sentiment is strong.

HAWAII AND OUR FUTURE SEA POWER.

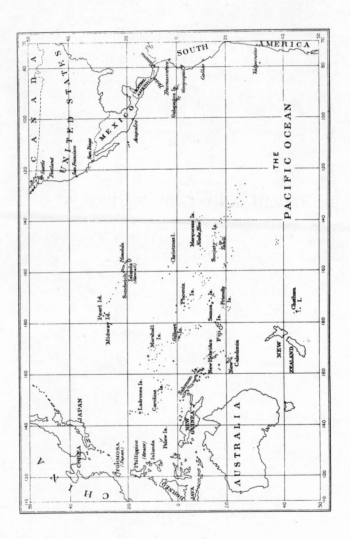

HAWAII AND OUR FUTURE SEA POWER.

[The origin of the ensuing article was as follows: At the
time of the Revolution in Hawaii, at the beginning of 1893, the
author addressed to the " New York Times " a letter, which
appeared in the issue of January 31. This, falling under the
eye of the Editor of the " Forum," suggested to him to ask an
article upon the general military — or naval — value of the
Hawaiian group.   The letter alluded to ran thus : —

To the Editor of the " New York Times " : —

There is one aspect of the recent revolution in Hawaii
which seems to have been kept out of sight, and that is the
relation of the islands, not merely to our own and to European
countries, but to China. How vitally important that may become in the future is evident from the great number of Chinese,
relatively to the whole population, now settled in the islands.

It is a question for the whole civilized world and not for the
United States only, whether the Sandwich Islands, with their
geographical and military importance, unrivalled by that of any
other position in the North Pacific, shall in the future be an outpost of European civilization, or of the comparative barbarism
of China. It is sufficiently known, but not, perhaps, generally
noted in our country, that many military men abroad, familiar
with Eastern conditions and character, look with apprehension
toward the day when the vast mass of China — now inert — may
yield to one of those impulses which have in past ages buried
civilization under a wave of barbaric invasion. The great armies
of Europe, whose existence is so frequently deplored, may be

providentially intended as a barrier to that great movement, if it come.   Certainly, while China remains as she is, nothing more disastrous for the future of the world can be imagined than that general disarmament of Europe which is the Utopian dream of some philanthropists.

China, however, may burst her barriers eastward as well as westward, toward the Pacific as well as toward the European Continent.   In such a movement it would be impossible to exaggerate the momentous issues dependent upon a firm hold of the Sandwich Islands by a great, civilized, maritime power. By its nearness to the scene, and by the determined animosity to the Chinese movement which close contact seems to inspire, our own country, with its Pacific coast, is naturally indicated as the proper guardian for this most important position.   To hold it, however, whether in the supposed case or in war with a European state, implies a great extension of our naval power. Are we ready to undertake this?

A. T. MAHAN,
Captain, United States Navy.

NEW YORK, Jan. 30, 1893.]

THE suddenness — so far, at least, as the general public is concerned — with which the long-existing troubles in Hawaii have come to a head, and the character of the advances reported to be addressed to the United States by the revolutionary government, formally recognized as *de facto* by our representative on the spot, add another to the many significant instances furnished by history, that, as men in the midst of life are in death, so nations in the midst of peace find themselves confronted with unexpected causes of dissension, conflicts of interests, whose results may be, on the one hand, war, or, on the other, abandonment of clear and imperative national advantage in order to avoid an issue for which preparation has not been made. By no premeditated contrivance of our own, by the co-operation of a series of events which, however dependent step by step upon human action, were not intended to prepare the present crisis, the United States finds herself compelled to answer a question — to make a decision — not unlike and not less momentous than that required of the Roman senate, when the Mamertine garrison invited it to occupy Messina, and so to abandon the hitherto traditional policy which had confined the expansion of Rome to the Italian peninsula. For let it not be overlooked that, whether we wish or no, we *must* answer the question, we *must* make the decision. The issue cannot be dodged. Absolute inaction in such a case is a decision as truly as the most vehement action. We can now advance, but, the conditions of the world being what they are, if we do not advance we recede; for there is involved not so much a particular

3

action as a question of principle, pregnant of great consequences in one direction or in the other.

Occasion of serious difficulty, indeed, should not arise here. Unlike the historical instance just cited, the two nations whose interests have come now into contact — Great Britain and the United States — are so alike in inherited traditions, habits of thought, and views of right, that injury to the one need not be anticipated from the predominance of the other in a quarter where its interests also predominate. Despite the heterogeneous character of the immigration which the past few years have been pouring into our country, our political traditions and racial characteristics still continue English — Mr. Douglas Campbell would say Dutch, but even so the stock is the same. Though thus somewhat gorged with food not wholly to its taste, our political digestion has contrived so far to master the incongruous mass of materials it has been unable to reject; and if assimilation has been at times imperfect, our political constitution and spirit remain English in essential features. Imbued with like ideals of liberty, of law, of right, cer-

tainly not less progressive than our kin beyond sea, we are, in the safeguards deliberately
placed around our fundamental law, even more
conservative than they. That which we received of the true spirit of freedom we have
kept — liberty and law — not the one or the
other, but both. In that spirit we not only
have occupied our original inheritance, but
also, step by step, as Rome incorporated the
other nations of the peninsula, we have added
to it, spreading and perpetuating everywhere
the same foundation principles of free and
good government which, to her honor be it
said, Great Britain also has maintained throughout her course. And now, arrested on the
south by the rights of a race wholly alien to
us, and on the north by a body of states of like
traditions to our own, whose freedom to choose
their own affiliations we respect, we have come
to the sea. In our infancy we bordered upon
the Atlantic only; our youth carried our boundary to the Gulf of Mexico; to-day maturity
sees us upon the Pacific. Have we no right
or no call to progress farther in any direction?
Are there for us beyond the sea horizon none
of those essential interests, of those evident

dangers, which impose a policy and confer rights?

This is the question that long has been looming upon the brow of a future now rapidly passing into the present. Of it the Hawaiian incident is a part — intrinsically, perhaps, a small part — but in its relations to the whole so vital that, as has been said before, a wrong decision does not stand by itself, but involves, not only in principle but in fact, recession along the whole line. In our natural, necessary, irrepressible expansion, we are come here into contact with the progress of another great people, the law of whose being has impressed upon it a principle of growth which has wrought mightily in the past, and in the present is visible by recurring manifestations. Of this working, Gibraltar, Malta, Cyprus, Egypt, Aden, India, in geographical succession though not in strict order of time, show a completed chain; forged link by link, by open force or politic bargain, but always resulting from the steady pressure of a national instinct, so powerful and so accurate that statesmen of every school, willing or unwilling, have found themselves carried along by a tendency which no individuality can resist or greatly modify. Both unsubstantial rumor and incautious personal utterance have suggested an impatient desire in Mr. Gladstone to be rid of the occupation of Egypt; but scarcely has his long exclusion from office ended when the irony of events signalizes his return thereto by an increase in the force of occupation. Further, it may be noted profitably of the chain just cited, that the two extremities were first possessed — first India, then Gibraltar, far later Malta, Aden, Cyprus, Egypt — and that, with scarce an exception, each step has been taken despite the jealous vexation of a rival. Spain has never ceased angrily to bewail Gibraltar. " I had rather see the English on the heights of Montmartre," said the first Napoleon, "than in Malta." The feelings of France about Egypt are matter of common knowledge, not even dissembled; and, for our warning be it added, her annoyance is increased by the bitter sense of opportunity rejected.

It is needless here to do more than refer to that other chain of maritime possessions — Halifax, Bermuda, Santa Lucia, Jamaica — which strengthen the British hold upon the Atlantic, the Caribbean, and the Isthmus of Panama. In the Pacific the position is for them much less satisfactory — nowhere, perhaps, is it less so, and from obvious natural causes. The commercial development of the eastern Pacific has been far later, and still is less complete, than that of its western shores. The latter when first opened to European adventure were already the seat of ancient economies in China and Japan, furnishing abundance of curious and luxurious products to tempt the trader by good hopes of profit. The western coast of America, for the most part peopled by savages, offered little save the gold and silver of Mexico and Peru, and these were monopolized jealously by the Spaniards — not a commercial nation — during their long ascendency. Being so very far from England and affording so little material for trade, Pacific America did not draw the enterprise of a country the chief and honorable inducement of whose seamen was the hope of gain, in pursuit of which they settled and annexed point after point in the regions where they penetrated, and upon the routes leading thither. The western coasts of North America, being reached only by the long

and perilous voyage around Cape Horn, or by
a more toilsome and dangerous passage across
the continent, remained among the last of the
temperate productive seaboards of the earth to
be possessed by white men. The United
States were already a nation, in fact as well as
in form, when Vancouver was exploring Puget
Sound and passed first through the channel
separating the mainland of British America
from the island which now bears his name.
Thus it has happened that, from the late development of British Columbia in the northeastern
Pacific, and of Australia and New Zealand
in the southwestern, Great Britain is found
again holding the two extremities of a line,
between which she must inevitably desire the
intermediate links; nor is there any good
reason why she should not have them, except
the superior, more urgent, more vital necessities of another people — our own. Of these
links the Hawaiian group possesses unique
importance — not from its intrinsic commercial value, but from its favorable position for
maritime and military control.

The military or strategic value of a naval
position depends upon its situation, upon its

strength, and upon its resources. Of the three, the first is of most consequence, because it results from the nature of things; whereas the two latter, when deficient, can be supplied artificially, in whole or in part. Fortifications remedy the weaknesses of a position, foresight accumulates beforehand the resources which nature does not yield on the spot; but it is not within the power of man to change the geographical situation of a point which lies outside the limit of strategic effect. It is instructive, and yet apparent to the most superficial reading, to notice how the first Napoleon, in commenting upon a region likely to be the scene of war, begins by considering the most conspicuous natural features, and then enumerates the commanding positions, their distances from each other, the relative directions, or, as the sea phrase is, their "bearings," and the particular facilities each offers for operations of war. This furnishes the ground plan, the skeleton, detached from confusing secondary considerations, and from which a clear estimate of the decisive points can be made. The number of such points varies greatly, according to the character of the region. In a mountainous, broken country they may be very many; whereas in a plain devoid of natural obstacles there may be few, or none save those created by man. If few, the value of each is necessarily greater than if many; and if there be but one, its importance is not only unique, but extreme, — measured only by the size c the field over which its unshared influence extends.

The sea, until it approaches the land, realizes the ideal of a vast plain unbroken by obstacles. On the sea, says an eminent French tactician, there is no field of battle, meaning that there is none of the natural conditions which determine, and often fetter, the movements of the general. But upon a plain, however flat and monotonous, causes, possibly slight, determine the concentration of population into towns and villages, and the necessary communications between the centres create roads. Where the latter converge, or cross, tenure confers command, depending for importance upon the number of routes thus meeting, and upon their individual value. It is just so at sea. While in itself the ocean opposes no obstacle to a vessel taking any one of the numerous routes that can be traced upon the surface of the globe between two points, conditions of distance or convenience, of traffic or of wind, do prescribe certain usual courses. Where these pass near an ocean position, still more where they use it, it has an influence over them, and where several routes cross near by that influence becomes very great, — is commanding.

Let us now apply these considerations to the Hawaiian group. To any one viewing a map that shows the full extent of the Pacific Ocean, with its shores on either side, two striking circumstances will be apparent immediately. He will see at a glance that the Sandwich Islands stand by themselves, in a state of comparative isolation, amid a vast expanse of sea ; and, again, that they form the centre of a large circle whose radius is approximately — and very closely — the distance from Honolulu to San Francisco. The circumference of this circle, if the trouble is taken to describe it with compass upon the map, will be seen, on the west and south, to pass through the outer fringe of the system of archipelagoes which, from Australia and New Zealand, extend to the northeast toward the American continent. Within the circle a few scattered islets, bare and unimportant, seem only to emphasize the failure of nature to bridge the interval separating Hawaii from her peers of the Southern Pacific. Of these, however, it may be noted that some, like Fanning and Christmas Islands, have within a few years been taken into British possession. The distance from San Francisco to Honolulu, twenty-one hundred miles — easy steaming distance — is substantially the same as that from Honolulu to the Gilbert, Marshall, Samoan, Society, and Marquesas groups, all under European control, except Samoa, in which we have a part influence.

To have a central position such as this, and to be alone, having no rival and admitting no alternative throughout an extensive tract, are conditions that at once fix the attention of the strategist, — it may be added, of the statesmen of commerce likewise. But to this striking combination are to be added the remarkable relations, borne by these singularly placed islands, to the greater commercial routes traversing this vast expanse known to us as the Pacific, — not only, however, to those now actually in use, important as they are, but also to those that must be called into being necessarily by that future to which the Hawaiian incident compels our too unwilling attention. Circumstances, as already remarked, create centres, between which communication necessarily follows; and in the vista of the future all discern, however dimly, a new and great centre that must largely modify existing sea routes, as well as bring new ones into existence. Whether the canal of the Central American isthmus be eventually at Panama or at Nicaragua matters little to the question now in hand, although, in common with most Americans who have thought upon the subject, I believe it surely will be at the latter point. Whichever it be, the convergence there of so many ships from the Atlantic and the Pacific will constitute a centre of commerce, interoceanic, and inferior to few, if to any, in the world; one whose approaches will be watched jealously, and whose relations to the other centres of the Pacific by the lines joining it to them must be examined carefully. Such study of the commercial routes and of their relations to the Hawaiian Islands, taken together with the other strategic considerations previously set forth, completes the synopsis of facts which determine the value of the group for conferring either commercial or naval control.

Referring again to the map, it will be seen that while the shortest routes from the Isthmus to Australia and New Zealand, as well as those to South America, go well clear of any probable connection with or interference from Hawaii, those directed toward China and Japan pass either through the group or in close proximity to it. Véssels from Central America bound to the ports of North America come, of course, within the influence of our own coast. These circumstances, and the existing recognized distribution of political power in the Pacific, point naturally to an international acquiescence in certain defined spheres of influence, for our own country and for others, such as has been reached already between Great Britain, Germany, and Holland in the Southwestern Pacific, to avoid conflict there between their respective claims. Though artificial in form, such a recognition, in the case here suggested, would depend upon perfectly natural as well as indisputable conditions.

The United States is by far the greatest, in numbers, interests, and power, of the communities bordering upon the eastern shores of the North Pacific; and the relations of the Hawaiian Islands to her naturally would be, and actually are, more numerous and more important than they can be to any other state. This is true, although, unfortunately for the equally natural wishes of Great Britain and her colonies, the direct routes from British Columbia to Eastern Australia and New Zealand, which depend upon no building of a future canal, pass as near the islands as those already mentioned. Such a fact, that this additional great highway runs close to the group, both augments and emphasizes their strategic importance; but it does not affect the statement just made, that the interest of the United States in them surpasses that of Great Britain, and dependent upon a natural cause, nearness, which has been admitted always as a reasonable ground for national self-assertion. It is unfortunate, doubtless, for the wishes of British Columbia, and for the communications, commercial and military, depending upon the Canadian Pacific Railway, that the United States lies between them and the South Pacific, and is the state nearest to Hawaii; but, the fact being so, the interests of our sixty-five million people, in a position so vital to our part in the Pacific, must be allowed to outweigh those of the six millions of Canada.

From the foregoing considerations may be inferred the importance of the Hawaiian Islands as a position powerfully influencing the commercial and military control of the Pacific, and especially of the Northern Pacific, in which the United States, geographically, has the strongest right to assert herself. These are the main advantages, which can be termed positive: those, namely, which directly advance commercial security and naval control. To the negative advantages of possession, by removing conditions which, if the islands were in the hands of any other power, would constitute to us disadvantages and threats, allusion only will be made. The serious menace to our Pacific coast and our Pacific trade, if so important a position were held by a possible enemy, has been mentioned frequently in the press, and dwelt upon in the diplomatic papers which from time to time are given to the public.

It may be assumed that it is generally acknowledged.   Upon one particular, however, too
much stress cannot be laid, one to which naval
officers cannot but be more sensitive than the
general public, and that is the immense disadvantage to us of any maritime enemy having
a coaling-station well within twenty-five hundred miles, as this is, of every point of our
coast-line from Puget Sound to Mexico.   Were
there many others available, we might find it
difficult to exclude from all.   There is, however, but the one.   Shut out from the Sandwich
Islands as a coal base, an enemy is thrown back
for supplies of fuel to distances of thirty-five
hundred or four thousand miles, — or between
seven thousand and eight thousand, going and
coming, — an impediment to sustained maritime operations well-nigh prohibitive.   The
coal-mines of British Columbia constitute, of
course, a qualification to this statement; but
upon them, if need arose, we might hope at
least to impose some trammels by action from
the land side.   It is rarely that so important a
factor in the attack or defence of a coast-line —
of a sea frontier — is concentrated in a single
position; and the circumstance renders doubly

imperative upon us to secure it, if we righteously can.

It is to be hoped, also, that the opportunity
thus thrust upon us may not be viewed narrowly, as though it concerned but one section
of our country or one portion of its external
trade or influence. This is no mere question
of a particular act, for which, possibly, just
occasion may not have offered yet; but of a
principle, a policy, fruitful of many future acts,
to enter upon which, in the fulness of our
national progress, the time now has arrived.
The principle being accepted, to be conditioned
only by a just and candid regard for the rights
and reasonable susceptibilities of other nations,
— none of which is contravened by the step
here immediately under discussion, — the annexation, even, of Hawaii would be no mere
sporadic effort, irrational because disconnected
from an adequate motive, but a first-fruit and
a token that the nation in its evolution has
aroused itself to the necessity of carrying its
life — that has been the happiness of those
under its influence — beyond the borders which
heretofore have sufficed for its activities. That
the vaunted blessings of our economy are not

4

to be forced upon the unwilling may be conceded; but the concession does not deny the
right nor the wisdom of gathering in those who
wish to come. Comparative religion teaches
that creeds which reject missionary enterprise
are foredoomed to decay. May it not be so
with nations? Certainly the glorious record of
England is consequent mainly upon the spirit,
and traceable to the time, when she launched
out into the deep — without formulated policy,
it is true, or foreseeing the future to which her
star was leading, but obeying the instinct which
in the infancy of nations anticipates the more
reasoned impulses of experience. Let us, too,
learn from her experience. Not all at once did
England become the great sea power which she
is, but step by step, as opportunity offered, she
has moved on to the world-wide pre-eminence
now held by English speech, and by institutions
sprung from English germs. How much
poorer would the world have been, had Englishmen heeded the cautious hesitancy that
now bids us reject every advance beyond our
shore-lines! And can any one doubt that a
cordial, if unformulated, understanding between
the two chief states of English tradition, to

spread freely, without mutual jealousy and in mutual support, would increase greatly the world's sum of happiness?

But if a plea of the world's welfare seem suspiciously like a cloak for national self-interest, let the latter be accepted frankly as the adequate motive which it assuredly is. Let us not shrink from pitting a broad self-interest against the narrow self-interest to which some would restrict us. The demands of our three great seaboards, the Atlantic, the Gulf, and the Pacific, — each for itself, and all for the strength that comes from drawing closer the ties between them, — are calling for the extension, through the Isthmian Canal, of that broad sea common along which, and along which alone, in all the ages prosperity has moved. Land carriage, always restricted and therefore always slow, toils enviously but hopelessly behind, vainly seeking to replace and supplant the royal highway of nature's own making. Corporate interests, vigorous in that power of concentration which is the strength of armies and of minorities, may here withstand for a while the ill-organized strivings of the multitude, only dimly conscious of its wants; yet the latter, however temporarily opposed and baffled, is sure at last, like the blind forces of nature, to overwhelm all that stand in the way of its necessary progress. So the Isthmian Canal is an inevitable part in the future of the United States; yet one that cannot be separated from other necessary incidents of a policy dependent upon it, whose details cannot be foreseen exactly. But because the precise steps that hereafter may be opportune or necessary cannot yet be foretold certainly, is not a reason the less, but a reason the more, for establishing a principle of action which may serve to guide as opportunities arise. Let us start from the fundamental truth, warranted by history, that the control of the seas, and especially along the great lines drawn by national interest or national commerce, is the chief among the merely material elements in the power and prosperity of nations. It is so because the sea is the world's great medium of circulation. From this necessarily follows the principle that, as subsidiary to such control, it is imperative to take possession, when it can be done righteously, of such maritime positions as contribute to secure command. If this principle be adopted, there will be no hesitation about taking the positions — and they are many — upon the approaches to the Isthmus, whose interests incline them to seek us. It has its application also to the present case of Hawaii.

There is, however, one caution to be given from the military point of view, beyond the need of which the world has not yet passed. Military positions, fortified posts, by land or by sea, however strong or admirably situated, do not confer control by themselves alone. People often say that such an island or harbor will give control of such a body of water. It is an utter, deplorable, ruinous mistake. The phrase indeed may be used by some only loosely, without forgetting other implied conditions of adequate protection and adequate navies; but the confidence of our own nation in its native strength, and its indifference to the defence of its ports and the sufficiency of its fleet, give reason to fear that the full consequences of a forward step may not be weighed soberly. Napoleon, who knew better, once talked this way. "The islands of San Pietro, Corfu, and Malta," he wrote, "will make us masters of the whole Mediterranean." Vain boast! Within one year Corfu, in two years Malta, were rent away from the state that could not support them by its ships. Nay, more: had Bonaparte not taken the latter stronghold out of the hands of its degenerate but innocuous government, that citadel of the Mediterranean would perhaps — would probably — never have passed into those of his chief enemy. There is here also a lesson for us.

It is by no means logical to leap, from this recognition of the necessity of adequate naval force to secure outlying dependencies, to the conclusion that the United States would need for that object a navy equal to the largest now existing. A nation as far removed as is our own from the bases of foreign naval strength may reasonably reckon upon the qualification that distance — not to speak of the complex European interests close at hand — impresses upon the exertion of naval strength by European powers. The mistake is when our remoteness, unsupported by carefully calculated force, is regarded as an armor of proof, under cover of which any amount of swagger may be indulged safely. An estimate of what is an adequate naval force for our country may properly take into account the happy interval which separates both our present territory and our future aspirations from the centres of interest really vital to European states. If to these safeguards be added, on our part, a sober recognition of what our reasonable sphere of influence is, and a candid justice in dealing with foreign interests within that sphere, there will be little disposition to question our preponderance therein.

Among all foreign states, it is especially to be hoped that each passing year may render more cordial the relations between ourselves and the great nation from whose loins we sprang. The radical identity of spirit which underlies our superficial differences of polity surely will draw us closer together, if we do not set our faces wilfully against a tendency which would give our race the predominance over the seas of the world. To force such a consummation is impossible, and if possible would not be wise; but surely it would be a lofty aim, fraught with immeasurable benefits, to desire it, and to raise no needless impediments by advocating perfectly proper acts, demanded by our evident interests, in offensive or arrogant terms.

THE ISTHMUS AND SEA POWER.

THE ISTHMUS AND SEA POWER.[1]

June, 1893.

FOR more than four hundred years the mind of man. has been possessed with a great idea, which, although by its wide diffusion and prophetic nature resembling one of those fundamental instincts, whose very existence points to a necessary fulfilment, first quickened into life in the thought of Christopher Columbus. To him the vision, dimly seen through the scanty and inaccurate knowledge of his age, imaged a close and facile communication, by means of the sea, that great bond of nations, between two ancient and diverse civilizations, which centred, the one around the Mediterranean, the birthplace of European commerce, refinement, and culture, the other upon the shores of that distant Eastern Ocean which lapped the dominions of the Great Khan, and held upon

[1] The Map of the Gulf and Caribbean, p. 271, will serve for geographical references of this article.

its breast the rich island of Zipangu. Hitherto an envious waste of land, entailing years of toilsome and hazardous journey, had barred them asunder. A rare traveller now and again might penetrate from one to the other, but it was impossible to maintain by land the constant exchange of influence and benefit which, though on a contracted scale, had constituted the advantage and promoted the development of the Mediterranean peoples. The microcosm of the land-girt sea typified then that future greater family of nations, which one by one have been bound since into a common tie of interest by the broad enfolding ocean, that severs only to knit them more closely together. So with a seer's eye, albeit as in a glass darkly, saw Columbus, and was persuaded, and embraced the assurance. As the bold adventurer, walking by faith and not by sight, launched his tiny squadron upon its voyage, making the first step in the great progress which was to be, and still is not completed, he little dreamed that the mere incident of stumbling upon an unknown region that lay across his route should be with posterity his chief title to fame, obscuring the true glory of his grand conception, as well as delaying its fulfilment to a far distant future.

The story of his actual achievement is sufficiently known to all readers, and need not be repeated here. Amid the many disappointments and humiliations which succeeded the brief triumphant blaze of his first return, and clouded the latter years of his life, Columbus was spared the pang of realizing that the problem was insoluble for the time. Like many a prophet before him, he knew not what, nor what manner of time, the spirit that was in him foretold, and died the happier for his ignorance. The certainty that a wilderness, peopled by savages and semi-barbarians, had been added to the known world, would have been a poor awakening from the golden dreams of beneficent glory as well as of profit which so long had beckoned him on. That the western land he had discovered interposed a barrier to the further progress of ships towards his longed-for goal, as inexorable as the mountain ranges and vast steppes of Asia, was mercifully concealed from his eyes; and the elusive "secret of the strait" through which he to the last hoped to pass, though tantalizing in its constant evasion, kept in tension the springs of hope and moral energy which might have succumbed under the knowledge of the truth.

It fell to the great discoverer, in his last voyage, to approach the continent, and to examine its shores along the region where the true secret of the strait lay hidden, — where, if ever, it shall pass from a dream to a reality, by the hand of man.   In the autumn of 1502, after many trials and misadventures, Columbus, having skirted the south side of Cuba, reached the north coast of Honduras.   There was little reason, except in his own unaccountable conviction, for continuing thence in one direction rather than in the other; but by some process of thought he had convinced himself that the sought-for strait lay to the south rather than to the north.   He therefore turned to the eastward, though the wind was contrary, and, after a hard buffet against it, doubled Cape Gracias á Dios, which still retains its expressive name, significant of his relief at finding that the trend of the beach at last permitted him to follow his desired course with a fair wind.   During the next two months

he searched the entire coast-line as far as
Porto Bello, discovering and examining several
openings in the land which since have been
of historical importance, among others the
mouth of the San Juan River and the Chiriqui
Lagoon, one of whose principal divisions still
recalls his visit in its name, Almirante Bay,
the Bay of the Admiral. A little beyond, to
the eastward of Porto Bello, he came to a
point already known to the Spaniards, having
been reached from Trinidad. The explorer
thus acquired the certainty that, from the
latter island to Yucatan, there was no break
in the obdurate shore which barred his access
to Asia.

Every possible site for an interoceanic canal
lies within the strip of land thus visited by
Columbus shortly before his death in 1504.
How narrow the insurmountable obstacle, and
how tantalizing, in the apparent facilities for
piercing it extended by the formation of the
land, were not known until ten years later,
when Balboa, led on by the reports of the
natives, reached the eminence whence he, first
among Europeans, saw the South Sea, — a
name long and vaguely applied to the Pacific,

because of the direction in which it lay from its discoverer. During these early years the history of the region we now know as Central America was one of constant strife among the various Spanish leaders, encouraged rather than stifled by the jealous home government; but it was also one of unbroken and venturesome exploration, a healthier manifestation of the same restless and daring energy that provoked their internal collisions. In January, 1522, one Gil Gonzalez started from Panama northward on the Pacific side, with a few frail barks, and in March discovered Lake Nicaragua, which has its name from the cacique, Nicaragua, or Nicarao, whose town stood upon its shores. Five years later, another adventurer took his vessel to pieces on the coast, transported it thus to the lake, and made the circuit of the latter; discovering its outlet, the San Juan, just a quarter of a century after Columbus had visited the mouth of the river.

The conquest of Peru, and the gradual extension of Spanish domination and settlements in Central America and along the shores of the Pacific, soon bestowed upon the Isthmus an importance, vividly suggestive of

its rise into political prominence consequent
upon the acquisition of California by the
United States, and upon the spread of the
latter along the Pacific coast. The length
and severity of the voyage round Cape Horn,
then as now, impelled men to desire some
shorter and less arduous route; and, inconvenient as the land transport with its repeated
lading and unlading was, it presented before
the days of steam the better alternative, as
to some extent it still does. So the Isthmus
and its adjoining regions became a great centre of commerce, a point where many highways
converged and whence they parted; where
the East and the West met in intercourse,
sometimes friendly, more often hostile. Thus
was realized partially, though most incompletely, the vision of Columbus; and thus, after
many fluctuations, and despite the immense
expansion of these latter days, partial and
incomplete his great conception yet remains.
The secret of the strait is still the problem
and the reproach of mankind.

By whatever causes produced, where such a
centre of commerce exists, there always will be
found a point of general interest to mankind,

— to all, at least, of those peoples who, whether directly commercial or not, share in the wide-spreading benefits and inconveniences arising from the fluctuations of trade. But enterprising commercial countries are not content to be mere passive recipients of these diverse influences. By the very characteristics which make them what they are, they are led perforce to desire, and to aim at, control of these decisive regions; for their tenure, like the key of a military position, exerts a vital effect upon the course of trade, and so upon the struggle, not only for bare existence, but for that increase of wealth, of prosperity, and of general consideration, which affect both the happiness and the dignity of nations. Consequently, in every age, according to its particular temperament and circumstances, there will be found manifested this desire for control; sometimes latent in an attitude of simple watchfulness; sometimes starting into vivid action under the impulse of national jealousies, and issuing in diplomatic rivalries or hostile encounter.

Such, accordingly, has been the history of the Central American Isthmus since the time when it became recognized as the natural cen-

tre, towards which, if not thwarted by adverse
influences, the current of intercourse between
East and West inevitably must tend. Here
the direction of least resistance was indicated
clearly by nature; and a concurrence of circumstances, partly inherent in the general
character of the region, partly adventitious or
accidental, contributed at an early date, and
until very recently, to emphasize and enlarge
the importance consequent upon the geographical situation and physical conformation
of this narrow barrier between two great seas.
For centuries the West India Islands, circling
the Caribbean, and guarding the exterior approaches to the Isthmus, continued to be the
greatest single source of tropical products
which had become increasingly necessary to
the civilized nations of Europe. In them, and
in that portion of the continent which extended on either side of the Isthmus, known
under the vague appellation of the Spanish
Main, Great Britain, during her desperate
strife with the first Napoleon, — a strife for
very existence, — found the chief support of
the commercial strength and credit that alone
carried her to the triumphant end. The Isth-

mus and the Caribbean were vital elements in determining the issue of that stern conflict. For centuries, also, the treasures of Mexico and Peru, upon which depended the vigorous action of the great though decadent military kingdom of Spain, flowed towards and accumulated around the Isthmus, where they were reinforced by the tribute of the Philippine Islands, and whence they took their way in the lumbering galleons for the ports of the Peninsula. Where factors of such decisive influence in European politics were at stake, it was inevitable that the rival nations, in peace as well as in open war, should carry their ambitions to the scene ; and the unceasing struggle for the mastery would fluctuate with the control of the waters, which, as in all maritime regions, must depend mainly upon naval preponderance, but also in part upon possession of those determining positions, of whose tenure Napoleon said that "war is a business of positions." Among these the Isthmus was chief.

The wild enterprises and bloody cruelties of the early buccaneers were therefore not merely a brutal exhibition of unpitying greed, indicative of the scum of nations as yet barely emerging from barbarism. They were this, doubtless, but they were something more. In the march of events, these early marauders played the same part, in relation to what was to succeed them, as the rude, unscrupulous, lawless adventurers who now precede the ruthless march of civilized man, who swarm over the border, occupy the outposts, and by their excesses stain the fair fame of the race whose pioneers they are. But, while thus libels upon and reproaches to the main body, they nevertheless belong to it, share its essential character, and foretell its inevitable course. Like driftwood swept forward on the crest of a torrent, they betoken the approaching flood. So with the celebrated freebooters of the Spanish Main. Of the same general type, — though varying greatly in individual characteristics, in breadth of view, and even in elevation of purpose, — their piratical careers not only evidenced the local wealth of the scene of their exploits, but attested the commercial and strategic importance of the position upon which in fact that wealth depended. The carcass was there, and the eagles as well as the vul-

tures, the far-sighted as well as the mere car-
rion birds of prey, were gathering round it.
" The spoil of Granada," said one of these mer-
cenary chieftains, two centuries ago, " I count
as naught beside the knowledge of the great
Lake Nicaragua, and of the route between the
Northern and Southern seas which depends
upon it."

As time passed, the struggle for the mastery
inevitably resulted, by a kind of natural selection, in the growing predominance of the people of the British Islands, in whom commercial
enterprise and political instinct were blended
so happily. The very lawlessness of the period
favored the extension of their power and influence; for it removed from the free play of a
nation's innate faculties the fetters which are
imposed by our present elaborate framework of
precedents, constitutions, and international law.
Admirably adapted as these are to the conservation and regular working of a political
system, they are, nevertheless, however wise,
essentially artificial, and hence are ill adapted
to a transition state, — to a period in which
order is evolving out of chaos, where the result
is durable exactly in proportion to the freedom

with which the natural forces are allowed to
act, and to reach their own equilibrium without
extraneous interference. Nor are such periods
confined to the early days of mere lawlessness.
They recur whenever a crisis is reached in the
career of a nation; when old traditions, accepted maxims, or written constitutions have
been outgrown, in whole or in part; when the
time has come for a people to recognize that
the limits imposed upon its expansion, by the
political wisdom of its forefathers, have ceased
to be applicable to its own changed conditions
and those of the world. The question then
raised is not whether the constitution, as written, shall be respected. It is how to reach
modifications in the constitution — and that
betimes — so that the genius and awakened
intelligence of the people may be free to act,
without violating that respect for its fundamental law upon which national stability ultimately
depends. It is a curious feature of our current
journalism that it is clear-sighted and prompt
to see the unfortunate trammels in which certain of our religious bodies are held, by the
cast-iron tenets imposed upon them by a past
generation, while at the same time political

tenets, similarly ancient, and imposed with a
like ignorance of a future which is our present,
are invoked freely to forbid this nation from
extending its power and necessary enterprise
into and beyond the seas, to which on every
side it now has attained.

During the critical centuries when Great
Britain was passing through that protracted
phase of her history in which, from one of the
least among states, she became, through the
power of the sea, the very keystone and foundation upon which rested the commercial —
for a time even the political — fabric of Europe,
the free action of her statesmen and people
was clogged by no uneasy sense that the national genius was in conflict with artificial,
self-imposed restrictions.   She plunged into
the brawl of nations that followed the discovery
of a new world, of an unoccupied if not un-
claimed inheritance, with a vigor and an initia-
tive which gained ever-accelerated momentum
and power as the years rolled by.   Far and
wide, in every sea, through every clime, her
seamen and her colonists spread; but while
their political genius and traditions enabled
them, in regions adapted to the physical well-

being of the race, to found self-governing colonies which have developed into one of the greatest of free states, they did not find, and never have found, that the possession of and rule over barbarous, or semi-civilized, or inert tropical communities, were inconsistent with the maintenance of political liberty in the mother country. The sturdy vigor of the broad principle of freedom in the national life is attested sufficiently by centuries of steady growth, that surest evidence of robust vitality. But, while conforming in the long run to the dictates of natural justice, no feeble scrupulosity impeded the nation's advance to power, by which alone its mission and the law of its being could be fulfilled. No artificial fetters were forged to cramp the action of the state, nor was it drugged with political narcotics to dwarf its growth.

In the region here immediately under consideration, Great Britain entered the contest under conditions of serious disadvantage. The glorious burst of maritime and colonial enterprise which marked the reign of Elizabeth, as the new era dawned when the country recognized the sphere of its true greatness, was confronted by the full power of Spain, as yet outwardly unshaken, in actual tenure of the most important positions in the Caribbean and the Spanish Main, and claiming the right to exclude all others from that quarter of the world. How brilliantly this claim was resisted is well known; yet, had they been then in fashion, there might have been urged, to turn England from the path which has made her what she is, the same arguments that now are freely used to deter our own country from even accepting such advantages as are ready to drop into her lap. If it be true that Great Britain's maritime policy now is imposed to some extent by the present necessities of the little group of islands which form the nucleus of her strength, it is not true that any such necessities first impelled her to claim her share of influence in the world, her part in the great drama of nations. Not for such reasons did she launch out upon the career which is perhaps the noblest yet run by any people. It then could have been said to her, as it now is said to us, " Why go beyond your own borders ? Within them you have what suffices for your needs and those of your population. There are mani-

fold abuses within to be corrected, manifold
miseries to be relieved.   Let the outside world
take care of itself.   Defend yourself, if attacked;
being, however, always careful to postpone
preparation to the extreme limit of imprudence.
'Sphere of influence,' 'part in the world,'
'national prestige,'—there are no such things;
or if there be, they are not worth fighting for."
What England would have been, had she so
reasoned, is matter for speculation; that the
world would have been poorer may be confidently affirmed.

As the strength of Spain waned apace during
the first half of the seventeenth century, the
external efforts of Great Britain also slackened
through the rise of internal troubles, which
culminated in the Great Rebellion, and absorbed for the time all the energies of the people.   The momentum acquired under Drake,
Raleigh, and their associates was lost, and an
occasion, opportune through the exhaustion of
the great enemy, Spain, passed unimproved.
But, though thus temporarily checked, the
national tendency remained, and quickly resumed its sway when Cromwell's mighty hand
had composed the disorders of the Common-

wealth. His clear-sighted statesmanship, as
well as the immediate necessities of his internal
policy, dictated the strenuous assertion by sea
of Great Britain's claims, not only to external
respect, which he rigorously exacted, but also
to her due share in influencing the world outside her borders. The nation quickly re-
sponded to his proud appeal, and received
anew the impulse upon the road to sea power
which never since has been relaxed. To him
were due the measures — not, perhaps, economically the wisest, judged by modern lights,
but more than justified by the conditions of his
times — which drew into English hands the
carrying trade of the world. The glories of the
British navy as an organized force date also
from his short rule; and it was he who, in
1655, laid a firm basis for the development of
the country's sea power in the Caribbean, by
the conquest of Jamaica, from a military stand-
point the most decisive of all single positions in
that sea for the control of the Isthmus. It is
true that the successful attempt upon this
island resulted from the failure of the leaders
to accomplish Cromwell's more immediate purpose of reducing Santo Domingo, — that in so

far the particular fortunate issue was of the nature of an accident; but this fact serves only to illustrate more emphatically that, when a general line of policy, whether military or political, is correctly chosen upon sound principles, incidental misfortunes or disappointments do not frustrate the conception. The sagacious, far-seeing motive, which prompted Cromwell's movement against the West Indian possessions of Spain, was to contest the latter's claim to the monopoly of that wealthy region; and he looked upon British extension in the islands as simply a stepping-stone to control upon the adjacent continent. It is a singular commentary upon the blindness of historians to the true secret of Great Britain's rise among the nations, and of the eminent position she so long has held, that writers so far removed from each other in time and characteristics as Hume and the late J. R. Green should detect in this far-reaching effort of the Protector, only the dulled vision of " a conservative and unspeculative temper misled by the strength of religious enthusiasm." " A statesman of wise political genius," according to them, would have fastened his eyes rather upon the growing power of

France, "and discerned the beginning of that great struggle for supremacy" which was fought out under Louis XIV. But to do so would have been only to repeat, by anticipation, the fatal error of that great monarch, which forever forfeited for France the control of the seas, in which the surest prosperity of nations is to be found; a mistake, also, far more ruinous to the island kingdom than it was to her continental rival, bitter though the fruits thereof have been to the latter. Hallam, with clearer insight, says: "When Cromwell declared against Spain, and attacked her West Indian possessions, there was little pretence, certainly, of justice, but not by any means, as I conceive, the impolicy sometimes charged against him. So auspicious was his star, that the very failure of that expedition obtained a more advantageous possession for England than all the triumphs of her former kings." Most true; but because his star was despatched in the right direction to look for fortune, — by sea, not by land.

The great aim of the Protector was checked by his untimely death, which perhaps also definitely frustrated a fulfilment, in the actual possession of the Isthmus, that in his strong hands might have been feasible. His idea, however, remained prominent among the purposes of the English people, as distinguished from their rulers; and in it, as has been said before, is to be recognized the significance of the exploits of the buccaneers, during the period of external debility which characterized the reigns of the second Charles and James. With William of Orange the government again placed itself at the head of the national aspirations, as their natural leader; and the irregular operations of the freebooters were merged in a settled national policy. This, although for a moment diverted from its course by temporary exigencies, was clearly formulated in the avowed objects with which, in 1702, the wise Dutchman entered upon the War of the Spanish Succession, the last great act of his political life. From the Peace of Utrecht, which closed this war in 1713, the same design was pursued with ever-increasing intensity, but with steady success, and with it was gradually associated the idea of controlling also the communication between the two oceans by way of the Isthmus. The best known instance of this, because of its connection with the great name of Nelson, was the effort made by him, in conjunction with a land force, in 1780, when still a simple captain, to take possession of the course of the San Juan River, and so of the interoceanic route through Lake Nicaragua. The attempt ended disastrously, owing partly to the climate, and partly to the strong series of works, numbering no less than twelve, which the Spaniards, duly sensible of the importance of the position, had constructed between the lake and the sea.

Difficulties such as were encountered by Nelson withstood Great Britain's advance throughout this region. While neither blind nor indifferent to the advantages conferred by actual possession, through which she had profited elsewhere abundantly, the prior and long-established occupation by Spain prevented her obtaining by such means the control she ardently coveted, and in great measure really exercised. The ascendency which made her, and still makes her, the dominant factor in the political system of the West Indies and the Isthmus resulted from her sea power, understood in its broadest sense. She was the great trader, source of supplies, and medium of intercourse between the various colonies themselves, and from them to the outer world; while the capital and shipping employed in this traffic were protected by a powerful navy, which, except on very rare occasions, was fully competent to its work. Thus, while unable to utilize and direct the resources of the countries, as she could have done had they been her own property, she secured the fruitful use and reaped the profit of such commercial transactions as were possible under the inert and narrow rule of the Spaniards. The fact is instructive, for the conditions to-day are substantially the same as those of a century ago. Possession still vests in states and races which have not attained yet the faculty of developing by themselves the advantages conferred by nature; and control will abide still with those whose ships, whose capital, whose traders support the industrial system of the region, provided these are backed by a naval force adequate to the demands of the military situation, rightly understood. To any foreign state, control at the Central American Isthmus means naval control, naval predominance, to which tenure of the land is at best but a convenient incident.

Such, in brief, was the general tendency of

6

events until the time when the Spanish colonial empire began to break up, in 1808–10, and the industrial system of the West India islands to succumb under the approaching abolition of slavery. The concurrence of these two decisive incidents, and the confusion which ensued in the political and economical conditions, rapidly reduced the Isthmus and its approaches to an insignificance from which the islands have not yet recovered. The Isthmus is partially restored. Its importance, however, depends upon causes more permanent, in the natural order of things, than does that of the islands, which, under existing circumstances, and under any circumstances that can be foreseen as yet, derive their consequence chiefly from the effect which may be exerted from them upon the tenure of the Isthmus. Hence the latter, after a period of comparative obscurity, again emerged into notice as a vital political factor, when the spread of the United States to the Pacific raised the question of rapid and secure communication between our two great seaboards. The Mexican War, the acquisition of California, the discovery of gold, and the mad rush to the diggings which followed, hastened, but by no means originated, the necessity for a settlement of the intricate problems involved, in which the United States, from its positions on the two seas, has the predominant interest. But, though predominant, ours is not the sole interest; though less vital, those of other foreign states are great and consequential; and, accordingly, no settlement can be considered to constitute an equilibrium, much less a finality, which does not effect our preponderating influence, and at the same time insure the natural rights of other peoples. So far as the logical distinction between commercial and political will hold, it may be said that our interest is both commercial and political, that of other states almost wholly commercial.

The same national characteristics that of old made Great Britain the chief contestant in all questions of maritime importance — with the Dutch in the Mediterranean, with France in the East Indies, and with Spain in the West — have made her also the exponent of foreign opposition to our own asserted interest in the Isthmus. The policy initiated by Cromwell, of systematic aggression in the Caribbean, and of naval expansion and organization, has resulted in a combination of naval force with

naval positions unequalled, though not wholly
unrivalled, in that sea. And since, as the great
sea carrier, Great Britain has a preponderating
natural interest in every new route open to
commerce, it is inevitable that she should scru-
tinize jealously every proposition for the modification of existing arrangements, conscious as
she is of power to assert her claims, in case
the question should be submitted to the last
appeal.

Nevertheless, although from the nature of
the occupations which constitute the welfare
of her people, as well as from the characteristics of her power, Great Britain seemingly
has the larger immediate stake in a prospective
interoceanic canal, it has been recognized
tacitly on her part, as on our side openly asserted, that the bearing of all questions of
Isthmian transit upon our national progress,
safety, and honor, is more direct and more
urgent than upon hers. That she has felt so
is plain from the manner in which she has
yielded before our tenacious remonstrances, in
cases where the control of the Isthmus was
evidently the object of her action, — as in the
matters of the tenure of the Bay Islands and

of the protectorate of the Mosquito Coast. Our superior interest appears also from the nature of the conditions which will follow from the construction of a canal. So far as these changes are purely commercial, they will operate to some extent to the disadvantage of Great Britain; because the result will be to bring our Atlantic seaboard, the frontier of a rival manufacturing and commercial state, much nearer to the Pacific than it now is, and nearer to many points of that ocean than is England. To make a rough general statement, easily grasped by a reader without the map before him, Liverpool and New York are at present about equidistant, by water, from all points on the west coast of America, from Valparaiso to British Columbia. This is due to the fact that, to go through the Straits of Magellan, vessels from both ports must pass near Cape St. Roque, on the east coast of Brazil, which is nearly the same distance from each. If the Nicaragua Canal existed, the line on the Pacific equidistant from the two cities named would pass, roughly, by Yokohama, Shanghai, Hong Kong, and Melbourne, or along the coasts of Japan, China, and eastern

Australia, — Liverpool, in this case, using the Suez Canal, and New York that of Nicaragua. In short, the line of equidistance would be shifted from the eastern shore of the Pacific to its western coast, and all points of that ocean east of Japan, China, and Australia — for example, the Hawaiian Islands — would be nearer to New York than to Liverpool.

A recent British writer has calculated that about one-eighth of the existing trade of the British Islands would be affected unfavorably by the competition thus introduced. But this result, though a matter of national concern, is political only in so far as commercial prosperity or adversity modifies a nation's current history ; that is, indirectly. The principal questions affecting the integrity or security of the British Empire are not involved seriously, for almost all of its component parts lie within the regions whose mutual bond of union and shortest line of approach are the Suez Canal. Nowhere has Great Britain so little territory at stake, nowhere has she such scanty possessions, as in the eastern Pacific, upon whose relations to the world at large, and to ourselves in particular, the Isthmian Canal will exert the greatest influence.

The chief political result of the Isthmian Canal will be to bring our Pacific coast nearer, not only to our Atlantic seaboard, but also to the great navies of Europe. Therefore, while the commercial gain, through an uninterrupted water carriage, will be large, and is clearly indicated by the acrimony with which a leading journal, apparently in the interest of the great transcontinental roads, has lately maintained the singular assertion that water transit is obsolete as compared with land carriage, it is still true that the canal will present an element of much weakness from the military point of view. Except to those optimists whose robust faith in the regeneration of human nature rejects war as an impossible contingency, this consideration must occasion serious thought concerning the policy to be adopted by the United States.

The subject, so far, has given rise only to diplomatic arrangement and discussion, within which it is permissible to hope it always may be confined; but the misunderstandings and protracted disputes that followed the Clayton-Bulwer Treaty, and the dissatisfaction with the existing status that still obtains among many of our people, give warning that our steps, as a nation, should be governed by some settled notions, too universally held to be set aside by a mere change of administration or caprice of popular will. Reasonable discussion, which tends, either by its truth or by its evident errors, to clarify and crystallize public opinion on so important a matter, never can be amiss.

This question, from an abstract, speculative phase of the Monroe Doctrine, took on the concrete and somewhat urgent form of security for our trans-Isthmian routes against foreign interference towards the middle of this century, when the attempt to settle it was made by the oft-mentioned Clayton-Bulwer Treaty, signed April 19, 1850. Great Britain was found then to be in possession, actual or constructive, of certain continental positions, and of some outlying islands, which would contribute not only to military control, but to that kind of political interference which experience has shown to be the natural consequence of the proximity of a strong power to a weak one. These positions depended upon, indeed their tenure originated in, the possession of Jamaica, thus justifying Cromwell's forecast. Of them, the Belize, a strip of coast two hundred miles long, on the Bay of Honduras, immediately south of Yucatan, was so far from the Isthmus proper, and so little likely to affect the canal question, that the American negotiator was satisfied to allow its tenure to pass unquestioned, neither admitting nor denying anything as to the rights of Great Britain thereto. Its first occupation had been by British freebooters, who "squatted" there a very few years after Jamaica fell. They went to cut logwood, succeeded in holding their ground against the efforts of Spain to dislodge them, and their right to occupancy and to fell timber was allowed afterwards by treaty. Since the signature of the Clayton-Bulwer Treaty, this "settlement," as it was styled in that instrument, has become a British "possession," by a convention with Guatemala contracted in 1859. Later, in 1862, the quondam "settlement" and recent "possession" was erected, by royal commission, into a full colony, subordinate to the government of Jamaica. Guatemala being a Central American state, this constituted a distinct advance of British dominion in Central America, contrary to the terms of our treaty.

A more important claim of Great Britain
was to the protectorate of the Mosquito Coast,
— a strip understood by her to extend from
Cape Gracias á Dios south to the San Juan
River. In its origin, this asserted right dif-
fered little from similar transactions between
civilized man and savages, in all times and all
places. In 1687, thirty years after the island
was acquired, a chief of the aborigines there
settled was carried to Jamaica, received some
paltry presents, and accepted British protection. While Spanish control lasted, a certain
amount of squabbling and fighting went on
between the two nations ; but when the questions arose between England and the United
States, the latter refused to acquiesce in the
so-called protectorate, which rested, in her opinion, upon no sufficient legal ground as against
the prior right of Spain, that was held to have
passed to Nicaragua when the latter achieved
its independence. The Mosquito Coast was
too close to the expected canal for its tenure
to be considered a matter of indifference. Similar ground was taken with regard to the Bay
Islands, Ruatan and others, stretching along
the south side of the Bay of Honduras, near

the coast of the republic of that name, and so uniting, under the control of the great naval power, the Belize to the Mosquito Coast. The United States maintained that these islands, then occupied by Great Britain, belonged in full right to Honduras.

Under these *de facto* conditions of British occupation, the United States negotiator, in his eagerness to obtain the recession of the disputed points to the Spanish-American republics, seems to have paid too little regard to future bearings of the subject. Men's minds also were dominated then, as they are now notwithstanding the intervening experience of nearly half a century, by the maxims delivered as a tradition by the founders of the republic who deprecated annexations of territory abroad. The upshot was that, in consideration of Great Britain's withdrawal from Mosquitia and the Bay Islands, to which, by our contention, she had no right, and therefore really yielded nothing but a dispute, we bound ourselves, as did she, without term, to acquire no territory in Central America, and to guarantee the neutrality not only of the contemplated canal, but of any other that might be constructed. A special article, the eighth, was incorporated in the treaty to this effect, stating expressly that the wish of the two governments was " not only to accomplish a particular object, but to establish a general principle."

Considerable delay ensued in the restoration of the islands and of the Mosquito Coast to Honduras and Nicaragua, — a delay attended with prolonged discussion and serious misunderstanding between the United States and Great Britain.   The latter claimed that, by the wording of the treaty, she had debarred herself only from future acquisitions of territory in Central America; whereas our government asserted, and persistently instructed its agents, that its understanding had been that an entire abandonment of all possession, present and future, was secured by the agreement.   It is difficult, in reading the first article, not to feel that, although the practice may have been perhaps somewhat sharp, the wording can sustain the British position quite as well as the more ingenuous confidence of the United States negotiator; an observation interesting chiefly as showing the eagerness on the one side, whose contention was the weaker in all save right, and the wariness on the other, upon whom present possession and naval power conferred a marked advantage in making a bargain. By 1860, however, the restorations had been made, and the Clayton-Bulwer Treaty since then has remained the international agreement, defining our relations to Great Britain on the Isthmus.

Of the subsequent wrangling over this unfortunate treaty, if so invidious a term may be applied to the dignified utterances of diplomacy, it is unnecessary to give a detailed account. Our own country cannot but regret and resent any formal stipulations which fetter its primacy of influence and control on the American continent and in American seas; and the concessions of principle over-eagerly made in 1850, in order to gain compensating advantages which our weakness could not extort otherwise, must needs cause us to chafe now, when we are potentially, though, it must be confessed sorrowfully, not actually, stronger by double than we were then. The interest of Great Britain still lies, as it then lay, in the maintenance of the treaty. So long as the United States jealously resents all foreign interference in the Isthmus, and at the same time takes no steps to formulate a policy or develop a strength that can give shape and force to her own pretensions, just so long will the absolute control over any probable contingency of the future rest with Great Britain, by virtue of her naval positions, her naval power, and her omnipresent capital.

A recent unofficial British estimate of the British policy at the Isthmus, as summarized in the Clayton-Bulwer Treaty, may here have interest: " In the United States was recognized a coming formidable rival to British trade. In the face of the estimated disadvantage to European trade in general, and that of Great Britain in particular, to be looked for from a Central American canal, British statesmen, finding their last attempt to control the most feasible route (by Nicaragua) abortive, accomplished the next best object in the interest of British trade. They cast the onus of building the canal on the people who would reap the greatest advantage from it, and who were bound to keep every one else out, but were at the same time very unlikely to undertake such a gigantic enterprise outside their own undeveloped territories for many a long year; while at the same time they skilfully handicapped that country in favor of British sea power by entering into a joint guarantee to respect its neutrality when built. This secured postponement of construction indefinitely, and yet forfeited no substantial advantage necessary to establish effective naval control in the interests of British carrying trade."

Whether this passage truly represents the deliberate purpose of successive British governments may be doubtful, but it is an accurate enough estimate of the substantial result, as long as our policy continues to be to talk loud and to do nothing, — to keep others out, while refusing ourselves to go in. We neutralize effectually enough, doubtless ; for we neutralize ourselves while leaving other powers to act efficiently whenever it becomes worth while.

In a state like our own, national policy means public conviction, else it is but as sounding brass and a tinkling cymbal. But public conviction is a very different thing from popular impression, differing by all that separates a rational process, resulting in manly resolve, from a weakly sentiment that finds occasional hysterical utterance. The Monroe Doctrine, as popularly apprehended and in-dorsed, is a rather nebulous generality, which has condensed about the Isthmus into a faint point of more defined luminosity. To those who will regard, it is the harbinger of the day, incompletely seen in the vision of the great discoverer, when the East and the West shall be brought into closer communion by the realization of the strait that baffled his eager search. But, with the strait, time has intro-duced a factor of which he could not dream, — a great nation midway between the West he knew and the East he sougnt, spanning the continent he unwittingly found, itself both East and West in one. To such a state, which in itself sums up the two conditions of Columbus's problem; to which the control of the strait is a necessity, if not of existence, at least of its full development and of its national security, who can deny the right to predominate in influence over a region so vital to it? None can deny save its own people; and they do it, — not in words, perhaps, but in act. For let it not be forgotten that failure to act at an opportune moment is action as real as, though less creditable than, the most strenuous positive effort.

Action, however, to be consistent and well proportioned, must depend upon well-settled conviction; and conviction, if it is to be reasonable, and to find expression in a sound and continuous national policy, must result from a careful consideration of present conditions in the light of past experiences. Here, unquestionably, strong differences of opinion will be manifested at first, both as to the true significance of the lessons of the past, and the manner of applying them to the present. Such differences need not cause regret. Their appearance is a sign of attention aroused; and when discussion has become general and animated, we may hope to see the gradual emergence of a sound and operative public sentiment. What is to be deprecated and feared is indolent drifting, in wilful blindness to the approaching moment when action must be taken; careless delay to remove fetters, if such there be in the Constitution or in traditional prejudice, which may prevent our seizing opportunity when it occurs. Whatever be the particular merits of the pending Hawaiian question, it scarcely can be denied that its discussion has revealed the existence, real or fancied, of such clogs upon our action, and of a painful disposition to consider each such occurrence as merely an isolated event, instead of being, as it is, a warning that the time has come when we must make up our minds upon a broad issue of national policy. That there should be two opinions is not bad, but it is very bad to halt long between them.

There is one opinion — which it is needless to say the writer does not share — that, because many years have gone by without armed collision with a great power, the teaching of the past is that none such can occur; and that, in fact, the weaker we are in organized military strength, the more easy it is for our opponents to yield our points. Closely associated with this view is the obstinate rejection of any political action which involves implicitly the projection of our physical power, if needed, beyond the waters that gird our shores. Because our reasonable, natural — it might almost be called moral — claim to

preponderant influence at the Isthmus heretofore has compelled respect, though reluctantly
conceded, it is assumed that no circumstances
can give rise to a persistent denial of it.

It appears to the writer — and to many
others with whom he agrees, though without
claim to represent them — that the true state
of the case is more nearly as follows : Since
our nation came into being, a century ago,
with the exception of a brief agitation about
the year 1850, — due to special causes, which,
though suggestive, were not adequate, and
summarized as to results in the paralyzing
Clayton-Bulwer Treaty, — the importance of
the Central American Isthmus has been merely
potential and dormant. But, while thus temporarily obscured, its intrinsic conditions of
position and conformation bestow upon it a
consequence in relation to the rest of the
world which is inalienable, and therefore, to
become operative, only awaits those changes
in external conditions that must come in the
fulness of time. The indications of such
changes are already sufficiently visible to challenge attention. The rapid peopling of our
territory entails at least two. The growth of

the Pacific States enhances the commercial
and political importance of the Pacific Ocean
to the world at large, and to ourselves in particular; while the productive energies of the
country, and its advent to the three seas,
impel it necessarily to seek outlet by them
and access to the regions beyond. Under such
conditions, perhaps not yet come, but plainly
coming, the consequence of an artificial waterway that shall enable the Atlantic coast to
compete with Europe, on equal terms as to
distance, for the markets of eastern Asia, and
shall shorten by two-thirds the sea route from
New York to San Francisco, and by one-
half that to Valparaiso, is too evident for
insistence.

In these conditions, not in European necessities, is to be found the assurance that the
canal will be made. Not to ourselves only,
however, though to ourselves chiefly, will it be
a matter of interest when completed. Many
causes will combine to retain in the line of
the Suez Canal the commerce of Europe with
the East; but to the American shores of the
Pacific the Isthmian canal will afford a much
shorter and easier access for a trade already of

noteworthy proportions. A weighty consideration also is involved in the effect upon British
navigation of a war which should endanger its
use of the Suez Canal. The power of Great
Britain to control the long route from Gibraltar to the Red Sea is seriously doubted by a
large and thoughtful body of her statesmen
and seamen, who favor dependence, in war,
upon that by the Cape of Good Hope. By
Nicaragua, however, would be shorter than by
the Cape to many parts of the East; and the
Caribbean can be safeguarded against distant
European states much more easily than the
line through the Mediterranean, which passes
close by their ports.

Under this increased importance of the Isthmus, we cannot safely anticipate for the future
the cheap acquiescence which, under very different circumstances, has been yielded in the
past to our demands. Already it is notorious
that European powers are betraying symptoms
of increased sensitiveness as to the value of
Caribbean positions, and are strengthening
their grip upon those they now hold. Moral
considerations undoubtedly count for more
than they did, and nations are more reluctant

to enter into war; but still, the policy of states is determined by the balance of advantages, and it behooves us to know what our policy is to be, and what advantages are needed to turn in our favor the scale of negotiations and the general current of events.

If the decision of the nation, following one school of thought, is that the weaker we are the more likely we are to have our way, there is little to be said. Drifting is perhaps as good a mode as another to reach that desirable goal. If, on the other hand, we determine that our interest and dignity require that our rights should depend upon the will of no other state, but upon our own power to enforce them, we must gird ourselves to admit that freedom of interoceanic transit depends upon predominance in a maritime region — the Caribbean Sea — through which pass all the approaches to the Isthmus. Control of a maritime region is insured primarily by a navy; secondarily, by positions, suitably chosen and spaced one from the other, upon which as bases the navy rests, and from which it can exert its strength. At present the positions of the Caribbean are occupied by foreign powers, nor may we, however disposed to acquisition, obtain them by means other than righteous; but a distinct advance will have been made when public opinion is convinced that we need them, and should not exert our utmost ingenuity to dodge them when flung at our head. If the Constitution really imposes difficulties, it provides also a way by which the people, if convinced, can remove its obstructions. A protest, however, may be entered against a construction of the Constitution which is liberal, by embracing all it can be constrained to imply, and then immediately becomes strict in imposing these ingeniously contrived fetters.

Meanwhile no moral obligation forbids developing our navy upon lines and proportions adequate to the work it may be called upon to do. Here, again, the crippling force is a public impression, which limits our potential strength to the necessities of an imperfectly realized situation. A navy "for defence only" is a popular catchword. When, if ever, people recognize that we have three seaboards, that the communication by water of one of them with the other two will depend in a not remote future upon a strategic position hundreds of miles distant from our nearest port, — the mouth of the Mississippi, — they will see also that the word " defence," already too narrowly understood, has its application at points far away from our own coast.

That the organization of military strength involves provocation to war is a fallacy, which the experience of each succeeding year now refutes. The immense armaments of Europe are onerous; but nevertheless, by the mutual respect and caution they enforce, they present a cheap alternative, certainly in misery, prob-ably in money, to the frequent devastating wars which preceded the era of general military preparation. Our own impunity has resulted, not from our weakness, but from the unimpor-tance to our rivals of the points in dispute, compared with their more immediate interests at home. With the changes consequent upon the canal, this indifference will diminish. We also shall be entangled in the affairs of the great family of nations, and shall have to ac-cept the attendant burdens. Fortunately, as regards other states, we are an island power, and can find our best precedents in the history of the people to whom the sea has been a nursing mother.

POSSIBILITIES OF AN ANGLO-AMERICAN REUNION.

POSSIBILITIES OF AN ANGLO-AMERICAN REUNION.

July, 1894.

[The following article was requested by the Editor of the "North American Review," as one of a number, by several persons, dealing with the question of a formal political connection, proposed by Mr. Andrew Carnegie, between the United States and the British Empire, for the advancement of the general interests of the English-speaking peoples. The projects advocated by previous writers embraced: 1, a federate union; 2, a merely naval union or alliance; or, 3, a defensive alliance of a kind frequent in political history.]

THE words "kinship" and "alliance" express two radically distinct ideas, and rest, for both the privileges and the obligations involved in them, upon foundations essentially different. The former represents a natural relation, the latter one purely conventional, — even though it may result from the feelings, the mutual interests, and the sense of incumbent duty attendant upon the other. In its very etymology, accordingly, is found implied that sense of constraint, of an artificial bond, that may prove a source, not only of strength, but of irksomeness as well. Its analogue in our social conditions is the marriage tie, — the strongest, doubtless, of all bonds when it realizes in the particular case the supreme affection of which our human nature is capable ; but likewise, as daily experience shows, the most fretting when, through original mistake or unworthy motive, love fails, and obligation alone remains.

Personally, I am happy to believe that the gradual but, as I think, unmistakable growth of mutual kindly feelings between Great Britain and the United States during these latter years — and of which the recent articles of Sir George Clarke and Mr. Arthur Silva White in the " North American Review " are pleasant indications — is a sure evidence that a common tongue and common descent are making themselves felt, and are breaking down the barriers of estrangement which have separated too long men of the same blood. There is seen here the working of kinship, — a wholly normal result of a common origin, the natural affection of children of the same descent, who have quarrelled and have been alienated with the proverbial bitterness of civil strife, but who all along have realized — or at the least have been dimly conscious — that such a state of things is wrong and harmful. As a matter of sentiment only, this reviving affection well might fix the serious attention of those who watch the growth of world questions, recognizing how far imagination and sympathy rule the world; but when, besides the powerful sentimental impulse, it is remembered that beneath considerable differences of political form there lie a common inherited political tradition and habit of thought, that the moral forces which govern and shape political development are the same in either people, the possibility of a gradual approach to concerted action becomes increasingly striking. Of all the elements of the civilization that has spread over Europe and America, none is so potent for good as that singular combination of two essential but opposing factors — of individual freedom with subjection to law — which finds its most vigorous working in Great Britain and the United States, its only exponents in which an approach to a due balance has been effected. Like other peoples, we also sway between the two, inclining now to one side, now to the other; but the departure from the normal in either direction is never very great.

There is yet another noteworthy condition common to the two states, which must tend to incline them towards a similar course of action in the future. Partners, each, in the great commonwealth of nations which share the blessings of European civilization, they alone, though in varying degrees, are so severed geographically from all existing rivals as to be exempt from the burden of great land armies; while at the same time they must depend upon the sea, in chief measure, for that intercourse with other members of the body upon which national well-being depends. How great an influence upon the history of Great Britain has been exerted by this geographical isolation is sufficiently understood. In her case the natural tendency has been increased abnormally by the limited territorial extent of the British Islands, which has forced the energies of their inhabitants to seek fields for action outside their own borders; but the figures quoted by Sir George Clarke sufficiently show that the same tendency, arising from the same cause, does exist and is operative in the United

States, despite the diversion arising from the immense internal domain not yet fully occupied, and the great body of home consumers which has been secured by the protective system. The geographical condition, in short, is the same in kind, though differing in degree, and must impel in the same direction. To other states the land, with its privileges and its glories, is the chief source of national prosperity and distinction. To Great Britain and the United States, if they rightly estimate the part they may play in the great drama of human progress, is intrusted a maritime interest, in the broadest sense of the word, which demands, as one of the conditions of its exercise and its safety, the organized force adequate to control the general course of events at sea; to maintain, if necessity arise, not arbitrarily, but as those in whom interest and power alike justify the claim to do so, the laws that shall regulate maritime warfare. This is no mere speculation, resting upon a course of specious reasoning, but is based on the teaching of the past. By the exertion of such force, and by the maintenance of such laws, and by these means only, Great Britain, in the beginning of this century, when she was the solitary power of the seas, saved herself from destruction, and powerfully modified for the better the course of history.

With such strong determining conditions combining to converge the two nations into the same highway, and with the visible dawn of the day when this impulse begins to find expression in act, the question naturally arises, What should be the immediate course to be favored by those who hail the growing light, and would hasten gladly the perfect day? That there are not a few who seek a reply to this question is evidenced by the articles of Mr. Carnegie, of Sir George Clarke, and of Mr. White, all appearing within a short time in the pages of the " North American Review." And it is here, I own, that, though desirous as any one can be to see the fact accomplished, I shrink from contemplating it, under present conditions, in the form of an alliance, naval or other. Rather I should say: Let each nation be educated to realize the length and breadth of its own interest in the sea; when that is done, the identity of these interests will become apparent. This identity cannot be established firmly in men's minds antecedent to the great teacher,

Experience; and experience cannot be had before that further development of the facts which will follow the not far distant day, when the United States people must again betake themselves to the sea and to external action, as did their forefathers alike in their old home and in the new.

There are, besides, questions in which at present doubt, if not even friction, might arise as to the proper sphere of each nation, agreement concerning which is essential to cordial co-operation; and this the more, because Great Britain could not be expected reasonably to depend upon our fulfilment of the terms of an alliance, or to yield in points essential to her own maritime power, so long as the United States is unwilling herself to assure the security of the positions involved by the creation of an adequate force. It is just because in that process of adjusting the parts to be played by each nation, upon which alone a satisfactory co-operation can be established, a certain amount of friction is probable, that I would avoid all premature striving for alliance, an artificial and possibly even an irritating method of reaching the desired end. Instead, I would dwell con-

tinually upon those undeniable points of
resemblance in natural characteristics, and in
surrounding conditions, which testify to common origin and predict a common destiny.
Cast the seed of this thought into the ground,
and it will spring and grow up, you know not
how, — first the blade, then the ear, then the
full corn in the ear. Then you may put in
your sickle and reap the harvest of political
result, which as yet is obviously immature.
How quietly and unmarked, like the slow processes of nature, such feelings may be wrought
into the very being of nations, was evidenced
by the sudden and rapid rising of the North at
the outbreak of our civil war, when the flag
was fired upon at Fort Sumter. Then was
shown how deeply had sunk into the popular
heart the devotion to the Union and the flag,
fostered by long dwelling upon the ideas, by
innumerable Fourth of July orations, often
doubtless vainglorious, sometimes perhaps gro-
tesque, but whose living force and overwhelming results were vividly apparent, as the fire
leaped from hearthstone to hearthstone throughout the Northern States. Equally in the South
was apparent how tenacious and compelling

was the grip which the constant insistence upon the predominant claim of the State upon individual loyalty had struck into the hearts of her sons. What paper bonds, treaties, or alliances could have availed then to hold together people whose ideals had drifted so far apart, whose interests, as each at that time saw them, had become so opposed?

Although I am convinced firmly that it would be to the interest of Great Britain and the United States, and for the benefit of the world, that the two nations should act together cordially on the seas, I am equally sure that the result not only must be hoped but also quietly waited for, while the conditions upon which such cordiality depends are being realized by men. All are familiar with the idea conveyed by the words "forcing process." There are things that cannot be forced, processes which cannot be hurried, growths which are strong and noble in proportion as they imbibe slowly the beneficent influence of the sun and air in which they are bathed. How far the forcing process can be attempted by an extravagant imagination, and what the inevitable recoil of the mind you seek to take by storm, is amus-

ingly shown by Mr. Carnegie's " Look Ahead,"
and by the demur thereto of so ardent a cham-
pion of Anglo-American alliance — on terms
which appear to me to be rational though premature — as Sir George Clarke. A country
with a past as glorious and laborious as that of
Great Britain, unprepared as yet, as a whole, to
take a single step forward toward reunion, is
confronted suddenly — as though the tempta-
tion must be irresistible — with a picture of
ultimate results which I will not undertake to
call impossible (who can say what is impossible?), but which certainly deprives the nation
of much, if not all, the hard-wrought achievement of centuries. Disunion, loss of national
identity, changes of constitution more than
radical, the exchange of a world-wide empire for
a subordinate part in a great federation, — such
may be the destiny of Great Britain in the distant future. I know not; but sure I am, were
I a citizen of Great Britain, the prospect would
not allure me now to move an inch in such a
direction. Surely in vain the net is spread in
the sight of any bird.

The suggestions of Sir George Clarke and of
Mr. White are not open to the reproach of

repelling those whom they seek to convince. They are clear, plain, business-like proposions, based upon indisputable reasons of mutual advantage, and in the case of the former quickened, as I have the pleasure of knowing through personal acquaintance, by a more than cordial good-will and breadth of view in all that relates to the United States. Avoiding criticism of details — of which I have little to offer — my objection to them is simply that I do not think the time is yet ripe. The ground is not prepared yet in the hearts and understandings of Americans, and I doubt whether in those of British citizens. Both proposals contemplate a naval alliance, though on differing terms. The difficulty is that the United States, as a nation, does not realize or admit as yet that it has any strong interest in the sea; and that the great majority of our people rest firmly in a belief, deep rooted in the political history of our past, that our ambitions should be limited by the three seas that wash our eastern, western, and southern coasts. For myself, I believe that this, once a truth, can be considered so no longer with reference even to the present — much less to a future so near that it scarcely needs a prophet's eye to read; but even if it be but a prejudice, it must be removed before a further step can be taken. In our country national policy, if it is to be steadfast and consistent, must be identical with public conviction. The latter, when formed, may remain long quiescent; but given the appointed time, it will spring to mighty action — aye, to arms — as did the North and the South under their several impulses in 1861.

It is impossible that one who sees in the sea — in the function which it discharges towards the world at large — the most potent factor in national prosperity and in the course of history, should not desire a change in the mental attitude of our countrymen towards maritime affairs. The subject presents itself not merely as one of national importance, but as one concerning the world's history and the welfare of mankind, which are bound up, so far as we can see, in the security and strength of that civilization which is identified with Europe and its offshoots in America. For what, after all, is our not unjustly vaunted European and American civilization? An oasis set in the midst of a desert of barbarism, rent with many intestine troubles, and ultimately dependent, not upon its mere elaboration of organization, but upon the power of that organization to express itself in a menacing and efficient attitude of physical force, sufficient to resist the numerically overwhelming, but inadequately organized hosts of outsiders. Under present conditions these are diked off by the magnificent military organizations of Europe, which also as yet cope successfully with the barbarians within. Of what the latter are capable — at least in will — we have from time to time, and not least of late, terrific warnings, to which men scarcely can shut their eyes and ears; but sufficient attention hardly is paid to the possible dangers from those outside, who are wholly alien to the spirit of our civilization; nor do men realize how essential to the conservation of that civilization is the attitude of armed watchfulness between nations, which is maintained now by the great states of Europe. Even if we leave out of consideration the invaluable benefit to society, in this age of insubordination and anarchy, that so large a number of youth, at the most impressionable age, receive the lessons of obedience, order, respect

for authority and law, by which military training conveys a potent antidote to lawlessness, it
still would remain a mistake, plausible but
utter, to see in the hoped-for subsidence of the
military spirit in the nations of Europe a pledge
of surer progress of the world towards universal
peace, general material prosperity, and ease.
That alluring, albeit somewhat ignoble, ideal is
not to be attained by the representatives of
civilization dropping their arms, relaxing the
tension of their moral muscle, and from fighting animals becoming fattened cattle fit only
for slaughter.

When Carthage fell, and Rome moved onward, without an equal enemy against whom to
guard, to the dominion of the world of Mediterranean civilization, she approached and gradually realized the reign of universal peace, broken
only by those intestine social and political dis-
sensions which are finding their dark analogues
in our modern times of infrequent war. As the
strife between nations of that civilization died
away, material prosperity, general cultivation
and luxury, flourished, while the weapons
dropped nervelessly from their palsied arms.
The genius of Cæsar, in his Gallic and Ger-

manic campaigns, built up an outside barrier, which, like a dike, for centuries postponed the inevitable end, but which also, like every artificial barrier, gave way when the strong masculine impulse which first created it had degenerated into that worship of comfort, wealth, and general softness, which is the ideal of the peace prophets of to-day. The wave of the invaders broke in, — the rain descended, the floods came, the winds blew, and beat upon the house, and it fell, because not founded upon the rock of virile reliance upon strong hands and brave hearts to defend what was dear to them.

Ease unbroken, trade uninterrupted, hardship done away, all roughness removed from life, — these are our modern gods; but can they deliver us, should we succeed in setting them up for worship? Fortunately, as yet we cannot do so. We may, if we will, shut our eyes to the vast outside masses of aliens to our civilization, now powerless because we still, with a higher material development, retain the masculine combative virtues which are their chief possession; but, even if we disregard them, the ground already shakes beneath our feet with physical menace of destruction from within, against which the only security is in constant readiness to contend. In the rivalries of nations, in the accentuation of differences, in the conflict of ambitions, lies the preservation of the martial spirit, which alone is capable of coping finally with the destructive forces that from outside and from within threaten to submerge all the centuries have gained.

It is not then merely, nor even chiefly, a pledge of universal peace that may be seen in the United States becoming a naval power of serious import, with clearly defined external ambitions dictated by the necessities of her interoceanic position; nor yet in the cordial co-operation, as of kindred peoples, that the future may have in store for her and Great Britain. Not in universal harmony, nor in fond dreams of unbroken peace, rest now the best hopes of the world, as involved in the fate of European civilization. Rather in the competition of interests, in that reviving sense of nationality, which is the true antidote to what is bad in socialism, in the jealous determination of each people to provide first for its own, of which the tide of protection rising throughout the world, whether economically an error or not, is so marked a symptom — in these jarring sounds which betoken that there is no immediate danger of the leading peoples turning their swords into ploughshares — are to be heard the assurance that decay has not touched yet the majestic fabric erected by so many centuries of courageous battling. In this same pregnant strife the United States doubtless will be led, by undeniable interests and aroused national sympathies, to play a part, to cast aside the policy of isolation which befitted her infancy, and to recognize that, whereas once to avoid European entanglement was essential to the development of her individuality, now to take her share of the travail of Europe is but to assume an inevitable task, an appointed lot, in the work of upholding the common interests of civilization. Our Pacific slope, and the Pacific colonies of Great Britain, with an instinctive shudder have felt the threat, which able Europeans have seen in the teeming multitudes of central and northern Asia; while their overflow into the Pacific Islands shows that not only westward by land, but also eastward by sea, the flood may sweep. I am not careful, however, to search into the details of a great movement, which indeed may never come, but whose possibility, in existing conditions, looms large upon the horizon of the future, and against which the only barrier will be the warlike spirit of the representatives of civilization. Whate'er betide, Sea Power will play in those days the leading part which it has in all history, and the United States by her geographical position must be one of the frontiers from which, as from a base of operations, the Sea Power of the civilized world will energize.

For this seemingly remote contingency preparation will be made, if men then shall be found prepared, by a practical recognition now of existing conditions — such as those mentioned in the opening of this paper — and acting upon that knowledge. Control of the sea, by maritime commerce and naval supremacy, means predominant influence in the world; because, however great the wealth product of the land, nothing facilitates the necessary exchanges as does the sea. The fundamental truth concerning the sea — perhaps we should rather say the water — is that it is Nature's great medium of communication. It is improbable that control ever again will be exercised, as once it was, by a single nation. Like the pettier interests of the land, it must be competed for, perhaps fought for. The greatest of the prizes for which nations contend, it too will serve, like other conflicting interests, to keep alive that temper of stern purpose and strenuous emulation which is the salt of the society of civilized states, whose unity is to be found, not in a flat identity of conditions — the ideal of socialism — but in a common standard of moral and intellectual ideas.

Also, amid much that is shared by all the nations of European civilization, there are, as is universally recognized, certain radical differences of temperament and character, which tend to divide them into groups having the marked affinities of a common origin. When, as frequently happens on land, the members of these groups are geographically near each other, the mere proximity seems, like similar electricities, to develop repulsions which render political variance the rule and political combination the exception. But when, as is the case with Great Britain and the United States, the frontiers are remote, and contact — save in Canada — too slight to cause political friction, the preservation, advancement, and predominance of the race may well become a political ideal, to be furthered by political combination, which in turn should rest, primarily, not upon cleverly constructed treaties, but upon natural affection and a clear recognition of mutual benefit arising from working together. If the spirit be there, the necessary machinery for its working will not pass the wit of the race to provide; and in the control of the sea, the beneficent instrument that separates us that we may be better friends, will be found the object that neither the one nor the other can master, but which may not be beyond the conjoined energies of the race. When, if ever, an Anglo-American alliance, naval or other, does come, may it be rather as a yielding to irresistible popular impulse than as a scheme, however ingeniously wrought, imposed by the adroitness of statesmen.

We may, however, I think, dismiss from our minds the belief, frequently advanced, and which is advocated so ably by Sir George Clarke, that such mutual support would tend in the future to exempt maritime commerce in general from the harassment which it hitherto has undergone in war. I shall have to try for special clearness here in stating my own views, partly because to some they may appear retrogressive, and also because they may be thought by others to contradict what I have said elsewhere, in more extensive and systematic treatment of this subject.

The alliance which, under one form or another, — either as a naval league, according to Sir George, or as a formal treaty, according to Mr. White, — is advocated by both writers, looks ultimately and chiefly to the contingency of war. True, a leading feature of either proposal is to promote good-will and avert causes of dissension between the two contracting parties; but even this object is sought largely in order that they may stand by each other firmly in case of difficulty with other states. Thus even war may be averted more surely; but, should it come, it would find the two united upon the ocean, consequently all-powerful there, and so possessors of that mastership of the general situation which the sea always has conferred upon its unquestioned rulers. Granting the union of hearts and hands, the supremacy, from my standpoint, logically follows. But why, then, if supreme, concede to an enemy immunity for his commerce? "Neither Great Britain nor America," says Sir George Clarke, though he elsewhere qualifies the statement, "can see in the commerce of other peoples an incentive to attack." Why not? For what purposes, primarily, do navies exist? Surely not merely to fight one another, — to gain what Jomini calls "the sterile glory" of fighting battles in order to win them. If navies, as all agree, exist for the protection of commerce, it inevitably follows that in war they must aim at depriving their enemy of that great resource; nor is it easy to conceive what broad military use they can subserve that at all compares with the protection and destruction of trade. This Sir George indeed sees, for he says elsewhere, "Only on the principle of doing the utmost injury to an enemy, with a view to hasten the issue of war, can commerce-destroying be justified;" but he fails, I think, to appreciate the full importance of this qualifying concession, and neither he nor Mr. White seems to admit the immense importance of commerce-destroying, as such.

The mistake of both, I think, lies in not keeping clearly in view — what both certainly perfectly understand — the difference between the *guerre-de-course*, which is inconclusive, and commerce-destroying (or commerce prevention) through strategic control of the sea by powerful navies. Some nations more than others, but all maritime nations more or less, depend for their prosperity upon maritime commerce, and probably upon it more than upon any other single factor. Either under their own flag or that of a neutral, either by foreign trade or coasting trade, the sea is the greatest of boons to such a state; and under every form its sea-borne trade is at the mercy of a foe decisively superior.

Is it, then, to be expected that such foe will forego such advantage, — will insist upon spending blood and money in fighting, or money in the vain effort of maintaining a fleet which, having nothing to fight, also keeps its hands off such an obvious means of crippling the opponent and forcing him out of his ports? Great Britain's navy, in the French wars, not only protected her own commerce, but also annihilated that of the enemy; and both conditions — not one alone — were essential to her triumph.

9

It is because Great Britain's sea power, though still superior, has declined relatively to that of other states, and is no longer supreme, that she has been induced to concede to neutrals the principle that the flag covers the goods. It is a concession wrung from relative weakness — or possibly from a mistaken humanitarianism; but, to whatever due, it is all to the profit of the neutral and to the loss of the stronger belligerent. The only justification, in policy, for its yielding by the latter, is that she can no longer, as formerly, bear the additional burden of hostility, if the neutral should ally himself to the enemy. I have on another occasion said that the principle that the flag covers the goods is forever secured — meaning thereby that, so far as present indications go, no one power would be strong enough at sea to maintain the contrary by arms.

In the same way it may be asserted quite confidently that the concession of immunity to what is unthinkingly called the " private property " of an enemy on the sea, will never be conceded by a nation or alliance confident in its own sea power. It has been the dream of the weaker sea belligerents in all ages; and their arguments for it, at the first glance plausible, are very proper to urge from their point of view. That arch-robber, the first Napoleon, who so remorselessly and exhaustively carried the principle of war sustaining war to its utmost logical sequence, and even in peace scrupled not to quarter his armies on subject countries, maintaining them on what, after all, was simply private property of foreigners, — even he waxes quite eloquent, and superficially most convincing, as he compares the seizure of goods at sea, so fatal to his empire, to the seizure of a wagon travelling an inland country road.

In all these contentions there lies, beneath the surface plausibility, not so much a confusion of thought as a failure to recognize an essential difference of conditions. Even on shore the protection of private property rests upon the simple principle that injury is not to be wanton, — that it is not to be inflicted when the end to be attained is trivial, or largely disproportionate to the suffering caused. For this reason personal property, not embarked in commercial venture, is respected in civilized maritime war. Conversely, as we all know, the rule on land is by no means invariable, and private property receives scant consideration when its appropriation or destruction serves the purposes of an enemy. The man who trudges the highway, cudgel in hand, may claim for his cudgel all the sacredness with which civilization invests property; but if he use it to break his neighbor's head, the respect for his property, as such, quickly disappears. Now, private property borne upon the seas is engaged in promoting, in the most vital manner, the strength and resources of the nation by which it is handled. When that nation becomes belligerent, the private property, so called, borne upon the seas, is sustaining the well-being and endurance of the nation at war, and consequently is injuring the opponent, to an extent exceeding all other sources of national power. In these days of war correspondents, most of us are familiar with the idea of the dependence of an army upon its communications, and we know, vaguely perhaps, but still we know, that to threaten or harm the communications of an army is one of the most common and effective devices of strategy. Why? Because severed from its base an army languishes and dies, and when threatened with

such an evil it must fight at whatever disadvantage. Well, is it not clear that maritime
commerce occupies, to the power of a maritime state, the precise nourishing function that
the communications of an army supply to the
army? Blows at commerce are blows at the
communications of the state; they intercept its
nourishment, they starve its life, they cut the
roots of its power, the sinews of its war. While
war remains a factor, a sad but inevitable factor, of our history, it is a fond hope that commerce can be exempt from its operations, because in very truth blows against commerce
are the most deadly that can be struck; nor is
there any other among the proposed uses of
a navy, as for instance the bombardment of
seaport towns, which is not at once more cruel
and less scientific. Blockade such as that
enforced by the United States Navy during
the Civil War, is evidently only a special phase
of commerce-destroying; yet how immense —
nay, decisive — its results!

It is only when effort is frittered away in the
feeble dissemination of the *guerre-de-course*, instead of being concentrated in a great combination to control the sea, that commerce-destroying

justly incurs the reproach of misdirected effort. It is a fair deduction from analogy, that two contending armies might as well agree to respect each other's communications, as two belligerent states to guarantee immunity to hostile commerce.

THE FUTURE IN RELATION TO AMERICAN NAVAL POWER.

THE FUTURE IN RELATION TO AMERICAN NAVAL POWER.

June, 1895.

THAT the United States Navy within the last dozen years should have been recast almost wholly, upon more modern lines, is not, in itself alone, a fact that should cause comment, or give rise to questions about its future career or sphere of action. If this country needs, or ever shall need, a navy at all, indisputably in 1883 the hour had come when the time-worn hulks of that day, mostly the honored but superannuated survivors of the civil war, should drop out of the ranks, submit to well-earned retirement or inevitable dissolution, and allow their places to be taken by other vessels, capable of performing the duties to which they themselves were no longer adequate.

It is therefore unlikely that there underlay this re-creation of the navy — for such in truth it was —any more recondite cause than the urgent necessity of possessing tools wholly fit for the work which war-ships are called upon to do. The thing had to be done, if the national fleet was to be other than an impotent parody of naval force, a costly effigy of straw. But, concurrently with the process of rebuilding, there has been concentrated upon the development of the new service a degree of attention, greater than can be attributed even to the voracious curiosity of this age of newsmongering and of interviewers. This attention in some quarters is undisguisedly reluctant and hostile, in others not only friendly but expectant, in both cases betraying a latent impression that there is, between the appearance of the new-comer and the era upon which we now are entering, something in common. If such coincidence there be, however, it is indicative not of a deliberate purpose, but of a commencing change of conditions, economical and political, throughout the world, with which sea power, in the broad sense of the phrase, will be associated closely; not, indeed, as the cause, nor even chiefly as a result, but rather as the leading characteristic of activities which shall cease to be mainly internal, and shall occupy themselves with the wider interests that concern the relations of states to the world at large. And it is just at this point that the opposing lines of feeling divide. Those who hold that our political interests are confined to matters within our own borders, and are unwilling to admit that circumstances may compel us in the future to political action without them, look with dislike and suspicion upon the growth of a body whose very existence indicates that nations have international duties as well as international rights, and that international complications will arise from which we can no more escape than the states which have preceded us in history, or those contemporary with us. Others, on the contrary, regarding the conditions and signs of these times, and the extra-territorial activities in which foreign states have embarked so restlessly and widely, feel that the nation, however greatly against its wish, may become involved in controversies not unlike those which in the middle of the century caused very serious friction, but which the generation that saw

the century open would have thought too remote for its concern, and certainly wholly
beyond its power to influence.

Religious creeds, dealing with eternal veri-
ties, may be susceptible of a certain per-
manency of statement; yet even here we in
this day have witnessed the embarrassments
of some religious bodies, arising from a traditional adherence to merely human formulas,
which reflect views of the truth as it appeared
to the men who framed them in the distant
past. But political creeds, dealing as they do
chiefly with the transient and shifting conditions of a world which is passing away continually, can claim no fixity of allegiance,
except where they express, not the policy of
a day, but the unchanging dictates of righteousness. And inasmuch as the path of ideal
righteousness is not always plain nor always
practicable; as expediency, policy, the choice
of the lesser evil, must control at times; as
nations, like men, will occasionally differ, honestly but irreconcilably, on questions of right,
— there do arise disputes where agreement
cannot be reached, and where the appeal must
be made to force, that final factor which under-

lies the security of civil society even more than it affects the relations of states. The well-balanced faculties of Washington saw this in his day with absolute clearness. Jefferson either would not or could not. That there should be no navy was a cardinal prepossession of his political thought, born of an exaggerated fear of organized military force as a political factor. Though possessed with a passion for annexation which dominated much of his political action, he prescribed as the limit of the country's geographical expansion the line beyond which it would entail the maintenance of a navy. Yet fate, ironical here as elsewhere in his administration, compelled the recognition that, unless a policy of total seclusion is adopted, — if even then, — it is not necessary to acquire territory beyond sea in order to undergo serious international complications, which could have been avoided much more easily had there been an imposing armed shipping to throw into the scale of the nation's argument, and to compel the adversary to recognize the impolicy of his course as well as what the United States then claimed to be its wrongfulness.

The difference of conditions between the United States of to-day and of the beginning of this century illustrates aptly how necessary it is to avoid implicit acceptance of precedents, crystallized into maxims, and to seek for the quickening principle which justified, wholly or in part, the policy of one generation, but whose application may insure a very different course of action in a succeeding age. When the century opened, the United States was not only a continental power, as she now is, but she was one of several, of nearly equal strength as far as North America was concerned, with all of whom she had differences arising out of conflicting interests, and with whom, moreover, she was in direct geographical contact, — a condition which has been recognized usually as entailing peculiar proneness to political friction; for, while the interests of two nations may clash in quarters of the world remote from either, there is both greater frequency and greater bitterness when matters of dispute exist near at home, and especially along an artificial boundary, where the inhabitants of each are directly in contact with the causes of the irritation.

It was therefore the natural and proper aim of the government of that day to abolish the sources of difficulty, by bringing all the territory in question under our own control, if it could be done by fair means. We consequently entered upon a course of action precisely such as a European continental state would have followed under like circumstances. In order to get possession of the territory in which our interests were involved, we bargained and manœuvred and threatened; and although Jefferson's methods were peaceful enough, few will be inclined to claim that they were marked by excess of scrupulousness, or even of adherence to his own political convictions. From the highly moral standpoint, the acquisition of Louisiana under the actual conditions — being the purchase from a government which had no right to sell, in defiance of the remonstrance addressed to us by the power who had ceded the territory upon the express condition that it should not so be sold, but which was too weak to enforce its just reclamation against both Napoleon and ourselves — reduces itself pretty much to a choice between overreaching and violence, as the less repulsive means of compassing an end in itself both desirable and proper; nor does the attempt, by strained construction, to wrest West Florida into the bargain give a higher tone to the transaction. As a matter of policy, however, there is no doubt that our government was most wise; and the transfer, as well as the incorporation, of the territory was facilitated by the meagreness of the population that went with the soil. With all our love of freedom, it is not likely that many qualms were felt as to the political inclinations of the people concerning their transfer of allegiance. In questions of great import to nations or to the world, the wishes, or interests, or technical rights, of minorities must yield, and there is not necessarily any more injustice in this than in their yielding to a majority at the polls.

While the need of continental expansion pressed thus heavily upon the statesmen of Jefferson's era, questions relating to more distant interests were very properly postponed. At the time that matters of such immediate importance were pending, to enter willingly upon the consideration of subjects our concern

in which was more remote, either in time or
place, would have entailed a dissemination of
attention and of power that is as greatly to be
deprecated in statesmanship as it is in the
operations of war. Still, while the government
of the day would gladly have avoided such
complications, it found, as have the statesmen
of all times, that if external interests exist,
whatsoever their character, they cannot be
ignored, nor can the measures which prudence
dictates for their protection be neglected with
safety. Without political ambitions outside
the continent, the commercial enterprise of the
people brought our interests into violent antag-
onism with clear, unmistakable, and vital interests of foreign belligerent states ; for we shall
sorely misread the lessons of 1812, and of the
events which led to it, if we fail to see that the
questions in dispute involved issues more immediately vital to Great Britain, in her then
desperate struggle, than they were to ourselves,
and that the great majority of her statesmen
and people, of both parties, so regarded them.
The attempt of our government to temporize
with the difficulty, to overcome violence by
means of peaceable coercion, instead of meeting

it by the creation of a naval force so strong as to be a factor of consideration in the international situation, led us into an avoidable war.

The conditions which now constitute the political situation of the United States, relatively to the world at large, are fundamentally different from those that obtained at the beginning of the century. It is not a mere question of greater growth, of bigger size. It is not only that we are larger, stronger, have, as it were, reached our majority, and are able to go out into the world. That alone would be a difference of degree, not of kind. The great difference between the past and the present is that we then, as regards close contact with the power of the chief nations of the world, were really in a state of political isolation which no longer exists. This arose from our geographical position — reinforced by the slowness and uncertainty of the existing means of intercommunication — and yet more from the grave preoccupation of foreign statesmen with questions of unprecedented and ominous importance upon the continent of Europe. A policy of isolation was for us then practicable, — though even then only partially. It was expedient, also, because we were weak, and in order to allow the individuality of the nation time to accentuate itself. Save the questions connected with the navigation of the Mississippi, collision with other peoples was only likely to arise, and actually did arise, from going beyond our own borders in search of trade. The reasons now evoked by some against our political action outside our own borders might have been used then with equal appositeness against our commercial enterprises. Let us stay at home, or we shall get into trouble. Jefferson, in truth, averse in principle to commerce as to war, was happily logical in his embargo system. It not only punished the foreigner and diminished the danger of international complications, but it kept our own ships out of harm's way; and if it did destroy trade, and cause the grass to grow in the streets of New York, the incident, if inconvenient, had its compensations, by repressing hazardous external activities.

Few now, of course, would look with composure upon a policy, whatever its ground, which contemplated the peaceable seclusion of this nation from its principal lines of commerce. In 1807, however, a great party accepted the alternative rather than fight, or even than create a force which might entail war, although more probably it would have prevented it. But would it be more prudent now to ignore the fact that we are no longer — however much we may regret it — in a position of insignificance or isolation, political or geographical, in any way resembling the times of Jefferson, and that from the changed conditions may result to us a dilemma similar to that which confronted him and his supporters? Not only have we grown, — that is a detail, — but the face of the world is changed, economically and politically. The sea, now as always the great means of communication between nations, is traversed with a rapidity and a certainty that have minimized distances. Events which under former conditions would have been distant and of small concern, now happen at our doors and closely affect us. Proximity, as has been noted, is a fruitful source of political friction, but proximity is the characteristic of the age. The world has grown smaller. Positions formerly distant have become to us of vital importance from their nearness. But, while distances have shortened, they remain for us water distances, and, however short, for political influence they must be traversed in the last resort by a navy, the indispensable instrument by which, when emergencies arise, the nation can project its power beyond its own shore-line.

Whatever seeming justification, therefore, there may have been in the transient conditions of his own day for Jefferson's dictum concerning a navy, rested upon a state of things that no longer obtains, and even then soon passed away. The War of 1812 demonstrated the usefulness of a navy, — not, indeed, by the admirable but utterly unavailing single-ship victories that illustrated its course, but by the prostration into which our seaboard and external communications fell, through the lack of a navy at all proportionate to the country's needs and exposure. The navy doubtless reaped honor in that brilliant sea struggle, but the honor was its own alone; only discredit accrued to the statesmen who, with such men to serve them, none the less left the country open to the humiliation of its harried coasts and blasted commerce. Never was there a more lustrous example of what Jomini calls " the sterile glory of fighting battles merely to win them." Except for the

prestige which at last awoke the country to the
high efficiency of the petty force we called our
navy, and showed what the sea might be to us,
never was blood spilled more uselessly than in
the frigate and sloop actions of that day.   They
presented no analogy to the outpost and recon-
noissance fighting, to the detached services, that
are not only inevitable but invaluable, in maintaining the *morale* of a military organization in
campaign.   They were simply scattered efforts,
without relation either to one another or to any
main body whatsoever, capable of affecting
seriously the issues of war, or, indeed, to any
plan of operations worthy of the name.

Not very long after the War of 1812, within
the space of two administrations, there came
another incident, epoch-making in the history
of our external policy, and of vital bearing on
the navy, in the enunciation of the Monroe
doctrine.   That pronouncement has been curi-
ously warped at times from its original scope
and purpose.   In its name have been put forth
theories so much at odds with the relations of
states, as hitherto understood, that, if they be
maintained seriously, it is desirable in the interests of exact definition that their supporters

advance some other name for them. It is not necessary to attribute finality to the Monroe doctrine, any more than to any other political dogma, in order to deprecate the application of the phrase to propositions that override or transcend it. We should beware of being misled by names, and especially where such error may induce a popular belief that a foreign state is outraging wilfully a principle to the defence of which the country is committed. We have been committed to the Monroe doctrine itself, not perhaps by any such formal assumption of obligations as cannot be evaded, but by certain precedents, and by a general attitude, upon the whole consistently maintained, from which we cannot recede silently without risk of national mortification. If seriously challenged, as in Mexico by the third Napoleon, we should hardly decline to emulate the sentiments so nobly expressed by the British government, when, in response to the emperors of Russia and France, it declined to abandon the struggling Spanish patriots to the government set over them by Napoleon: " To Spain his Majesty is not bound by any formal instrument; but his Majesty has, in the face of the world, contracted with that nation engagements not less sacred, and not less binding upon his Majesty's mind, than the most solemn treaties." We may have to accept also certain corollaries which may appear naturally to result from the Monroe doctrine, but we are by no means committed to some propositions which lately have been tallied with its name. Those propositions possibly embody a sound policy, more applicable to present conditions than the Monroe doctrine itself, and therefore destined to succeed it; but they are not the same thing. There is, however, something in common between it and them. Reduced to its barest statement, and stripped of all deductions, natural or forced, the Monroe doctrine, if it were not a mere political abstraction, formulated an idea to which in the last resort effect could be given only through the instrumentality of a navy; for the gist of it, the kernel of the truth, was that the country had at that time distant interests on the land, political interests of a high order in the destiny of foreign territory, of which a distinguishing characteristic was that they could be assured only by sea.

Like most stages in a nation's progress, the

Monroe doctrine, though elicited by a particular political incident, was not an isolated step
unrelated to the past, but a development. It
had its antecedents in feelings which arose before our War of Independence, and which in
1778, though we were then in deadly need of
the French alliance, found expression in the
stipulation that France should not attempt to
regain Canada. Even then, and also in 1783,
the same jealousy did not extend to the Flori-
das, which at the latter date were ceded by
Great Britain to Spain; and we expressly ac-
quiesced in the conquest of the British West
India Islands by our allies. From that time
to 1815 no remonstrance was made against the
transfer of territories in the West Indies and
Caribbean Sea from one belligerent to another
— an indifference which scarcely would be
shown at the present time, even though the
position immediately involved were intrinsically of trivial importance; for the question at
stake would be one of principle, of consequences, far reaching as Hampden's tribute of
ship-money.

It is beyond the professional province of a
naval officer to inquire how far the Monroe

doctrine itself would logically carry us, or how far it may be developed, now or hereafter, by the recognition and statement of further national interests, thereby formulating another and wider view of the necessary range of our political influence. It is sufficient to quote its enunciation as a fact, and to note that it was the expression of a great national interest, not merely of a popular sympathy with South American revolutionists; for, had it been the latter, it would doubtless have proved as inoperative and evanescent as declarations arising from such emotions commonly are. From generation to generation we have been much stirred by the sufferings of Greeks, or Bulgarians, or Armenians, at the hands of Turkey; but, not being ourselves injuriously affected, our feelings have not passed into acts, and for that very reason have been ephemeral. No more than other nations are we exempt from the profound truth enunciated by Washington — seared into his own consciousness by the bitter futilities of the French alliance in 1778 and the following years, and by the extravagant demands based upon it by the Directory during his Presidential term — that it is absurd to expect governments to

act upon disinterested motives. It is not as an
utterance of passing concern, benevolent or selfish, but because it voiced an enduring principle of necessary self-interest, that the Monroe
doctrine has retained its vitality, and has been
made so easily to do duty as the expression of
intuitive national sensitiveness to occurrences
of various kinds in regions beyond the sea.
At its christening the principle was directed
against an apprehended intervention in American affairs, which depended not upon actual
European concern in the territory involved,
but upon a purely political arrangement between certain great powers, itself the result of
ideas at the time moribund. In its first application, therefore, it was a confession that danger of European complications did exist, under
conditions far less provocative of real European
interest than those which now obtain and are
continually growing. Its subsequent applica-
tions have been many and various, and the
incidents giving rise to them have been increasingly important, culminating up to the
present in the growth of the United States to
be a great Pacific power, and in her probable
dependence in the near future upon an Isth-

mian canal for the freest and most copious intercourse between her two ocean seaboards. In the elasticity and flexibleness with which the dogma thus has accommodated itself to varying conditions, rather than in the strict wording of the original statement, is to be seen the essential characteristic of a living principle — the recognition, namely, that not merely the interests of individual citizens, but the interests of the United States as a nation, are bound up with regions beyond the sea, not part of our own political domain, in which therefore, under some imaginable circumstances, we may be forced to take action.

It is important to recognize this, for it will help clear away the error from a somewhat misleading statement frequently made, — that the United States needs a navy for defence only, adding often, explanatorily, for the defence of our own coasts. Now in a certain sense we all want a navy for defence only. It is to be hoped that the United States will never seek war except for the defence of her rights, her obligations, or her necessary interests. In that sense our policy may always be defensive only, although it may compel us at

times to steps justified rather by expediency
— the choice of the lesser evil — than by in-
controvertible right. But if we have interests
beyond sea which a navy may have to protect,
it plainly follows that the navy has more to do,
even in war, than to defend the coast; and it
must be added as a received military axiom
that war, however defensive in moral character,
must be waged aggressively if it is to hope for
success.

For national security, the correlative of a
national principle firmly held and distinctly
avowed is, not only the will, but the power to
enforce it. The clear expression of national
purpose, accompanied by evident and adequate
means to carry it into effect, is the surest safe-
guard against war, provided always that the
national contention is maintained with a candid and courteous consideration of the rights
and susceptibilities of other states. On the
other hand, no condition is more hazardous
than that of a dormant popular feeling, liable
to be roused into action by a moment of
passion, such as that which swept over the
North when the flag was fired upon at Sumter,
but behind which lies no organized power for

action. It is on the score of due preparation for such an ultimate contingency that nations, and especially free nations, are most often deficient. Yet, if wanting in definiteness of foresight and persistency of action, owing to the inevitable frequency of change in the governments that represent them, democracies seem in compensation to be gifted with an instinct, the result perhaps of the free and rapid interchange of thought by which they are characterized, that intuitively and unconsciously assimilates political truths, and prepares in part for political action before the time for action has come. That the mass of United States citizens do not realize understandingly that the nation has vital political interests beyond the sea is probably true; still more likely is it that they are not tracing any connection between them and the reconstruction of the navy. Yet the interests exist, and the navy is growing; and in the latter fact is the best surety that no breach of peace will ensue from the maintenance of the former.

It is, not, then the indication of a formal political purpose, far less of anything like a threat, that is, from my point of view, to be recognized in the recent development of the navy. Nations, as a rule, do not move with the foresight and the fixed plan which distinguish a very few individuals of the human race. They do not practise on the pistol-range before sending a challenge; if they did, wars would be fewer, as is proved by the present long-continued armed peace in Europe. Gradually and imperceptibly the popular feeling, which underlies most lasting national movements, is aroused and swayed by incidents, often trivial, but of the same general type, whose recurrence gradually moulds public opinion and evokes national action, until at last there issues that settled public conviction which alone, in a free state, deserves the name of national policy. What the origin of those particular events whose interaction establishes a strong political current in a particular direction, it is perhaps unprofitable to inquire. Some will see in the chain of cause and effect only a chapter of accidents, presenting an interesting philosophical study, and nothing more; others, equally persuaded that nations do not effectively shape their mission in the world, will find in them the ordering of a Divine ruler, who does not

permit the individual or the nation to escape
its due share of the world's burdens. But,
however explained, it is a common experience
of history that in the gradual ripening of
events there comes often suddenly and unex-
pectedly the emergency, the call for action, to
maintain the nation's contention. That there
is an increased disposition on the part of civilized countries to deal with such cases by
ordinary diplomatic discussion and mutual
concession can be gratefully acknowledged ;
but that such dispositions are not always sufficient to reach a peaceable solution is equally
an indisputable teaching of the recent past.
Popular emotion, once fairly roused, sweeps
away the barriers of calm deliberation, and is
deaf to the voice of reason. That the consideration of relative power enters for much in
the diplomatic settlement of international difficulties is also certain, just as that it goes for
much in the ordering of individual careers.
" Can," as well as " will," plays a large share in
the decisions of life.

Like each man and woman, no state lives to
itself alone, in a political seclusion resembling
the physical isolation which so long was the

ideal of China and Japan. All, whether they
will or no, are members of a community, larger
or smaller; and more and more those of the
European family to which we racially belong are
touching each other throughout the world, with
consequent friction of varying degree. That
the greater rapidity of communication afforded
by steam has wrought, in the influence of sea
power over the face of the globe, an extension
that is multiplying the points of contact and
emphasizing the importance of navies, is a fact,
the intelligent appreciation of which is daily
more and more manifest in the periodical
literature of Europe, and is further shown by
the growing stress laid upon that arm of military strength by foreign governments; while
the mutual preparation of the armies on the
European continent, and the fairly settled territorial conditions, make each state yearly
more wary of initiating a contest, and thus
entail a political quiescence there, except in
the internal affairs of each country. The field
of external action for the great European
states is now the world, and it is hardly doubtful that their struggles, unaccompanied as
yet by actual clash of arms, are even under

that condition drawing nearer to ourselves. Coincidently with our own extension to the Pacific Ocean, which for so long had a good international claim to its name, that sea has become more and more the scene of political development, of commercial activities and rivalries, in which all the great powers, ourselves included, have a share. Through these causes Central and Caribbean America, now intrinsically unimportant, are brought in turn into great prominence, as constituting the gateway between the Atlantic and Pacific when the Isthmian canal shall have been made, and as guarding the approaches to it. The appearance of Japan as a strong ambitious state, resting on solid political and military foundations, but which scarcely has reached yet a condition of equilibrium in international standing, has fairly startled the world; and it is a striking illustration of the somewhat sudden nearness and unforeseen relations into which modern states are brought, that the Hawaiian Islands, so interesting from the international point of view to the countries of European civilization, are occupied largely by Japanese and Chinese.

In all these questions we have a stake, reluctantly it may be, but necessarily, for our evident interests are involved, in some instances directly, in others by very probable implication. Under existing conditions, the opinion that we can keep clear indefinitely of embarrassing problems is hardly tenable; while war between two foreign states, which in the uncertainties of the international situation throughout the world may break out at any time, will increase greatly the occasions of possible collision with the belligerent countries, and the consequent perplexities of our statesmen seeking to avoid entanglement and to maintain neutrality.

Although peace is not only the avowed but for the most part the actual desire of European governments, they profess no such aversion to distant political enterprises and colonial acquisitions as we by tradition have learned to do. On the contrary, their committal to such divergent enlargements of the national activities and influence is one of the most pregnant facts of our time, the more so that their course is marked in the case of each state by a persistence of the same national traits that characterized the great era of colonization, which followed the termination of the religious wars in Europe, and led to the world-wide contests of the eighteenth century. In one nation the action is mainly political, — that of a government pushed, by long-standing tradition and by its passion for administration, to extend the sphere of its operations so as to acquire a greater field in which to organize and dominate, somewhat regardless of economical advantage. In another the impulse comes from the restless, ubiquitous energy of the individual citizens, singly or in companies, moved primarily by the desire of gain, but carrying ever with them, subordinate only to the commercial aim, the irresistible tendency of the race to rule as well as to trade, and dragging the home government to recognize and to assume the consequences of their enterprise. Yet again there is the movement whose motive is throughout mainly private and mercantile, in which the individual seeks wealth only, with little or no political ambition, and where the government intervenes chiefly that it may retain control of its subjects in regions where but for such intervention they would become estranged from it. But, however diverse the modes of operation, all have a common characteristic, in that they bear the stamp of the national genius, — a proof that the various impulses are not artificial, but natural, and that they therefore will continue until an adjustment is reached.

What the process will be, and what the conclusion, it is impossible to foresee; but that friction at times has been very great, and matters dangerously near passing from the communications of cabinets to the tempers of the peoples, is sufficiently known. If, on the one hand, some look upon this as a lesson to us to keep clear of similar adventures, on the other hand it gives a warning that not only do causes of offence exist which may result at an unforeseen moment in a rupture extending to many parts of the world, but also that there is a spirit abroad which yet may challenge our claim to exclude its action and interference in any quarter, unless it finds us prepared there in adequate strength to forbid it, or to exercise our own. More and more civilized man is needing and seeking ground to occupy, room over which to expand and in which to live. Like all natural forces, the impulse takes the direction of least resistance, but when in its course it comes upon some region rich in possibilities, but unfruitful through the incapacity or negligence of those who dwell therein, the incompetent race or system will go down, as the inferior race ever has fallen back and disappeared before the persistent impact of the superior. The recent and familiar instance of Egypt is entirely in point. The continuance of the existing system — if it can be called such — had become impossible, not because of the native Egyptians, who had endured the like for ages, but because there were involved therein the interests of several European states, of which two principally were concerned by present material interest and traditional rivalry. Of these one, and that the one most directly affected, refused to take part in the proposed interference, with the result that this was not abandoned, but carried out solely by the other, which remains in political and administrative control of the country. Whether the original enterprise or the continued presence of Great Britain in Egypt is entirely clear of technical wrongs, open to the criticism of the pure moralist, is as little to the point as the morality of an earthquake; the general action was justified by broad considerations of moral expediency, being to the benefit of the world at large, and of the people of Egypt in particular — however they might have voted in the matter.

But what is chiefly instructive in this occurrence is the inevitableness, which it shares in common with the great majority of cases where civilized and highly organized peoples have trespassed upon the technical rights of possession of the previous occupants of the land — of which our own dealings with the American Indian afford another example. The inalienable rights of the individual are entitled to a respect which they unfortunately do not always get; but there is no inalienable right in any community to control the use of a region when it does so to the detriment of the world at large, of its neighbors in particular, or even at times of its own subjects. Witness, for example, the present angry resistance of the Arabs at Jiddah to the remedying of a condition of things which threatens to propagate a deadly disease far and wide, beyond the locality by which it is engendered; or consider the

horrible conditions under which the Armenian
subjects of Turkey have lived and are living.
When such conditions obtain, they can be prolonged only by the general indifference or mutual jealousies of the other peoples concerned —
as in the instance of Turkey — or because there
is sufficient force to perpetuate the misrule, in
which case the right is inalienable only until
its misuse brings ruin, or until a stronger force
appears to dispossess it.   It is because so
much of the world still remains in the possession of the savage, or of states whose imperfect
development, political or economical, does not
enable them to realize for the general use
nearly the result of which the territory is
capable, while at the same time the redundant
energies of civilized states, both government
and peoples, are finding lack of openings and
scantiness of livelihood at home, that there
now obtains a condition of aggressive restlessness with which all have to reckon.

That the United States does not now share
this tendency is entirely evident.   Neither her
government nor her people are affected by it
to any great extent.   But the force of circumstances has imposed upon her the necessity,

recognized with practical unanimity by her people, of insuring to the weaker states of America, although of racial and political antecedents different from her own, freedom to develop politically along their own lines and according to their own capacities, without interference in that respect from governments foreign to these continents. The duty is self-assumed; and resting, as it does, not upon political philanthropy, but simply upon our own proximate interests as affected by such foreign interference, has towards others rather the nature of a right than a duty. But, from either point of view, the facility with which the claim has been allowed heretofore by the great powers has been due partly to the lack of pressing importance in the questions that have arisen, and partly to the great latent strength of our nation, which was an argument more than adequate to support contentions involving matters of no greater immediate moment, for example, than that of the Honduras Bay Islands or of the Mosquito Coast. Great Britain there yielded, it is true, though reluctantly and slowly; and it is also true that, so far as organized force is concerned, she could have destroyed our navy then existing and otherwise have injured us greatly; but the substantial importance of the question, though real, was remote in the future, and, as it was, she made a political bargain which was more to her advantage than ours. But while our claim thus far has received a tacit acquiescence, it remains to be seen whether it will continue to command the same if the states whose political freedom of action we assert make no more decided advance towards political stability than several of them have done yet, and if our own organized naval force remains as slender, comparatively, as it once was, and even yet is. It is probably safe to say that an undertaking like that of Great Britain in Egypt, if attempted in this hemisphere by a non-American state, would not be tolerated by us if able to prevent it; but it is conceivable that the moral force of our contention might be weakened, in the view of an opponent, by attendant circumstances, in which case our physical power to support it should be open to no doubt.

That we shall seek to secure the peaceable solution of each difficulty as it arises is attested by our whole history, and by the disposition of

our people; but to do so, whatever the steps
taken in any particular case, will bring us into
new political relations and may entail serious
disputes with other states. In maintaining the
justest policy, the most reasonable influence,
one of the political elements, long dominant,
and still one of the most essential, is military
strength — in the broad sense of the word
"military," which includes naval as well — not
merely potential, which our own is, but organized and developed, which our own as yet is
not. We wisely quote Washington's warning
against entangling alliances, but too readily
forget his teaching about preparation for war.
The progress of the world from age to age, in
its ever-changing manifestations, is a great
political drama, possessing a unity, doubtless,
in its general development, but in which, as
act follows act, one situation alone can engage,
at one time, the attention of the actors. Of
this drama war is simply a violent and tumult-
uous political incident. A navy, therefore,
whose primary sphere of action is war, is, in the
last analysis and from the least misleading
point of view, a political factor of the utmost
importance in international affairs, one more

often deterrent than irritant.   It is in that light, according to the conditions of the age and of the nation, that it asks and deserves the appreciation of the state, and that it should be developed in proportion to the reasonable possibilities of the political future.

PREPAREDNESS FOR NAVAL WAR.

PREPAREDNESS FOR NAVAL WAR.

December, 1896.

THE problem of preparation for war in modern times is both extensive and complicated. As in the construction of the individual ship, where the attempt to reconcile conflicting requirements has resulted, according to a common expression, in a compromise, the most dubious of all military solutions, — giving something to all, and all to none, — so preparation for war involves many conditions, often contradictory one to another, at times almost irreconcilable. To satisfy all of these passes the ingenuity of the national Treasury, powerless to give the whole of what is demanded by the representatives of the different elements, which, in duly ordered proportion, constitute a complete scheme of national military policy, whether for offence or defence. Unable to satisfy all, and too often equally unable to say, frankly, " This one is chief; to it you others must yield, except so far as you contribute to its greatest efficiency," either the pendulum of the government's will swings from one extreme to the other, or, in the attempt to be fair all round, all alike receive less than they ask, and for their theoretical completeness require. In other words, the contents of the national purse are distributed, instead of being concentrated upon a leading conception, adopted after due deliberation, and maintained with conviction.

The creation of material for war, under modern conditions, requires a length of time which does not permit the postponement of it to the hour of impending hostilities. To put into the water a first-class battle-ship, fully armored, within a year after the laying of her keel, as has been done latterly in England, is justly considered an extraordinary exhibition of the nation's resources for naval shipbuilding; and there yet remained to be done the placing of her battery, and many other matters of principal detail essential to her readiness for sea. This time certainly would not be less for ourselves, doing our utmost.

War is simply a political movement, though violent and exceptional in its character. However sudden the occasion from which it arises, it results from antecedent conditions, the general tendency of which should be manifest long before to the statesmen of a nation, and to at least the reflective portion of the people. In such anticipation, such forethought, as in the affairs of common life, lies the best hope of the best solution, — peace by ordinary diplomatic action; peace by timely agreement, while men's heads are cool, and the crisis of fever has not been reached by the inflammatory utterances of an unscrupulous press, to which agitated public apprehension means increase of circulation. But while the maintenance of peace by sagacious prevision is the laurel of the statesman, which, in failing to achieve except by force, he takes from his own brow and gives to the warrior, it is none the less a necessary part of his official competence to recognize that in public disputes, as in private, there is not uncommonly on both sides an element of right, real or really believed, which prevents either party from yielding, and that it is better for men to fight than, for the

12

sake of peace, to refuse to support their convictions of justice. How deplorable the war between the North and South! but more deplorable by far had it been that either had flinched from the maintenance of what it believed to be fundamental right. On questions of merely material interest men may yield; on matters of principle they may be honestly in the wrong; but a conviction of right, even though mistaken, if yielded without contention, entails a deterioration of character, except in the presence of force demonstrably irresistible — and sometimes even then. Death before dishonor is a phrase which at times has been abused infamously, but it none the less contains a vital truth.

To provide a force adequate to maintain the nation's cause, and to insure its readiness for immediate action in case of necessity, are the responsibility of the government of a state, in its legislative and executive functions. Such a force is a necessary outcome of the political conditions which affect, or, as can be foreseen, probably may affect, the international relations of the country. Its existence at all and its size are, or should be, the reflection of the national consciousness that in this, that, or the other direction lie clear national interests — for which each generation is responsible to futurity — or national duties, equally clear from the mere fact that the matter lies at the door, like Lazarus at the rich man's gate. The question of when or how action shall be taken which may result in hostilities, is indeed a momentous one, having regard to the dire evils of war ; but it is the question of a moment, of the last moment to which can be postponed a final determination of such tremendous consequence. To this determination preparation for war has only this relation : that it should be adequate to the utmost demand that then can be made upon it, and, if possible, so imposing that it will prevent war ensuing, upon the firm presentation of demands which the nation believes to be just. Such a conception, so stated, implies no more than defence, — defence of the nation's rights or of the nation's duties, although such defence may take the shape of aggressive action, the only safe course in war.

Logically, therefore, a nation which proposes to provide itself with a naval or military organization adequate to its needs, must begin by considering, not what is the largest army or navy in the world, with the view of rivalling it, but what there is in the political status of the world, including not only the material interests but the temper of nations, which involves a reasonable, even though remote, prospect of difficulties which may prove insoluble except by war. The matter, primarily, is political in character. It is not until this political determination has been reached that the data for even stating the military problem are in hand; for here, as always, the military arm waits upon and is subservient to the political interests and civil power of the state.

It is not the most probable of dangers, but the most formidable, that must be selected as measuring the degree of military precaution to be embodied in the military preparations thenceforth to be maintained. The lesser is contained in the greater; if equal to the most that can be apprehended reasonably, the country can view with quiet eye the existence of more imminent, but less dangerous complications. Nor should it be denied that in estimating danger there should be a certain sobriety of imagination, equally removed from undue

confidence and from exaggerated fears. Napoleon's caution to his marshals not to make a
picture to themselves — not to give too loose
rein to fancy as to what the enemy might do,
regardless of the limitations to which military
movements are subject — applies to antecedent calculations, like those which we are considering now, as really as to the operations of
the campaign. When British writers, realizing
the absolute dependence of their own country
upon the sea, insist that the British navy must
exceed the two most formidable of its possible
opponents, they advance an argument which
is worthy at least of serious debate ; but when
the two is raised to three, they assume conditions which are barely possible, but lie too
far without the limits of probability to affect
practical action.

In like manner, the United States, in estimating her need of military preparation of
whatever kind, is justified in considering, not
merely the utmost force which might be
brought against her by a possible enemy, under
the political circumstances most favorable to
the latter, but the limitations imposed upon
an opponent's action by well-known conditions

of a permanent nature. Our only rivals in
potential military strength are the great powers
of Europe. These, however, while they have
interests in the western hemisphere, — to which
a certain solidarity is imparted by their instinctive and avowed opposition to a policy
to which the United States, by an inward compulsion apparently irresistible, becomes more and
more committed, — have elsewhere yet wider
and more onerous demands upon their attention. Since 1884 Great Britain, France, and
Germany have each acquired colonial possessions, varying in extent from one million to
two and a half million square miles, — chiefly
in Africa. This means, as is generally understood, not merely the acquisition of so much
new territory, but the perpetuation of national
rivalries and suspicions, maintaining in full
vigor, in this age, the traditions of past ani-
mosities. It means uncertainties about boun-
daries — that most fruitful source of disputes
when running through unexplored wildernesses
— jealousy of influence over native occupants
of the soil, fear of encroachment, unperceived
till too late, and so a constant, if silent, strife
to insure national preponderance in these

newly opened regions. The colonial expansion of the seventeenth and eighteenth centuries is being resumed under our eyes, bringing with it the same train of ambitions and feelings that were exhibited then, though these are qualified by the more orderly methods of modern days and by a well-defined mutual apprehension, — the result of a universal preparedness for war, the distinctive feature of our own time which most guarantees peace.

All this reacts evidently upon Europe, the common mother-country of these various foreign enterprises, in whose seas and lands must be fought out any struggle springing from these remote causes, and upon whose inhabitants chiefly must fall both the expense and the bloodshed thence arising. To these distant burdens of disquietude — in the assuming of which, though to an extent self-imposed, the present writer recognizes the prevision of civilization, instinctive rather than conscious, against the perils of the future — is to be added the proximate and unavoidable anxiety dependent upon the conditions of Turkey and its provinces, the logical outcome of centuries of Turkish misrule. Deplorable as have been,

and to some extent still are, political conditions on the American continents, the New
World, in the matter of political distribution
of territory and fixity of tenure, is permanence
itself, as compared with the stormy prospect
confronting the Old in its questions which will
not down.

In these controversies, which range themselves under the broad heads of colonial expansion and the Eastern question, all the
larger powers of Europe, the powers that maintain considerable armies or navies, or both, are
directly and deeply interested — except Spain.
The latter manifests no solicitude concerning
the settlement of affairs in the east of Europe,
nor is she engaged in increasing her still considerable colonial dominion. This preoccupation of the great powers, being not factitious,
but necessary, — a thing that cannot be dismissed by an effort of the national will, because its existence depends upon the nature of
things, — is a legitimate element in the military calculations of the United States. It cannot enter into her diplomatic considerations,
for it is her pride not to seek, from the embarrassments of other states, advantages or

concessions which she cannot base upon the substantial justice of her demands. But, while this is true, the United States has had in the past abundant experience of disputes, in which, though she believed herself right, even to the point of having a just *casus belli*, the other party has not seemed to share the same conviction. These difficulties, chiefly, though not solely, territorial in character, have been the natural bequest of the colonial condition through which this hemisphere passed on its way to its present political status. Her own view of right, even when conceded in the end, has not approved itself at first to the other party to the dispute. Fortunately these differences have been mainly with Great Britain, the great and beneficent colonizer, a state between which and ourselves a sympathy, deeper than both parties have been ready always to admit, has continued to exist, because founded upon common fundamental ideas of law and justice. Of this the happy termination of the Venezuelan question is the most recent but not the only instance.

It is sometimes said that Great Britain is the most unpopular state in Europe. If this be so,

— and many of her own people seem to accept the fact of her political isolation, though with more or less of regret, — is there nothing significant to us in that our attitude towards her in the Venezuelan matter has not commanded the sympathy of Europe, but rather the reverse? Our claim to enter, as of right, into a dispute not originally our own, and concerning us only as one of the American group of nations, has been rejected in no doubtful tones by organs of public opinion which have no fondness for Great Britain. Whether any foreign government has taken the same attitude is not known, — probably there has been no official protest against the apparent admission of a principle which binds nobody but the parties to it. Do we ourselves realize that, happy as the issue of our intervention has been, it may entail upon us greater responsibilities, more serious action, than we have assumed before? that it amounts in fact — if one may use a military metaphor — to occupying an advanced position, the logical result very likely of other steps in the past, but which nevertheless implies necessarily such organization of strength as will enable us to hold it?

Without making a picture to ourselves, without conjuring up extravagant contingencies, it is not difficult to detect the existence of conditions, in which are latent elements of future disputes, identical in principle with those through which we have passed heretofore. Can we expect that, if unprovided with adequate military preparation, we shall receive from other states, not imbued with our traditional habits of political thought, and therefore less patient of our point of view, the recognition of its essential reasonableness which has been conceded by the government of Great Britain? The latter has found capacity for sympathy with our attitude, — not only by long and close contact and interlacing of interests between the two peoples, nor yet only in a fundamental similarity of character and institutions. Besides these, useful as they are to mutual understanding, that government has an extensive and varied experience, extending over centuries, of the vital importance of distant regions to its own interests, to the interests of its people and its commerce, or to its political prestige. It can understand and allow for a determination not to acquiesce in the beginning or continuance of a state of things, the tendency of which is to induce future embarrassments, — to complicate or to endanger essential welfare. A nation situated as Great Britain is in India and Egypt scarcely can fail to appreciate our own sensitiveness regarding the Central American isthmus, and the Pacific, on which we have such extensive territory; nor is it a long step from concern about the Mediterranean, and anxious watchfulness over the progressive occupation of its southern shores, to an understanding of our reluctance to see the ambitions and conflicts of another hemisphere approach, even remotely and indirectly, the comparatively peaceful neighborhoods surrounding the Caribbean Sea, bearing a threat of disturbance to the political distribution of power or of territorial occupation now existing. Whatever our interests may demand in the future may be a matter of doubt, but it is hard to see how there can be any doubt in the mind of a British statesman that it is our clear interest now, when all is quiet, to see removed possibilities of trouble which might break out at a less propitious season.

Such facility for reaching an understanding,

due to experience of difficulties, is supported strongly by a hearty desire for peace, traditional with a commercial people who have not to reproach themselves with any lack of resolution or tenacity in assuming and bearing the burden of war when forced upon them. " Militarism " is not a preponderant spirit in either Great Britain or the United States; their commercial tendencies and their isolation concur to exempt them from its predominance. Pugnacious, and even warlike, when aroused, the idea of war in the abstract is abhorrent to them, because it interferes with their leading occupations, and its demands are alien to their habits of thought. To say that either lacks sensitiveness to the point of honor would be to wrong them ; but the point must be made clear to them, and it will not be found in the refusal of reasonable demands, because they involve the abandonment of positions hastily or ignorantly assumed, nor in the mere attitude of adhering to a position lest there may be an appearance of receding under compulsion. Napoleon I. phrased the extreme position of militarism in the words, " If the British ministry should intimate that there was anything the First Consul had not done, *because he was prevented from doing it*, that instant he would do it."

Now the United States, speaking by various organs, has said, in language scarcely to be misunderstood, that she is resolved to resort to force, if necessary, to prevent the territorial or political extension of European power beyond its present geographical limits in the American continents. In the question of a disputed boundary she has held that this resolve — dependent upon what she conceives her reasonable policy — required her to insist that the matter should be submitted to arbitration. If Great Britain should see in this political stand the expression of a reasonable national policy, she is able, by the training and habit of her leaders, to accept it as such, without greatly troubling over the effect upon men's opinions that may be produced by the additional announcement that the policy is worth fighting for, and will be fought for if necessary. It would be a matter of course for her to fight for her just interests, if need be, and why should not another state say the same? The point — of honor, if you like — is not whether a nation will fight, but whether its claim is just. Such an attitude, however, is not the spirit of "militarism," nor accordant with it; and in nations saturated with the military spirit, the intimation that a policy will be supported by force raises that sort of point of honor behind which the reasonableness of the policy is lost to sight. It can no longer be viewed dispassionately; it is prejudged by the threat, however mildly that be expressed. And this is but a logical development of their institutions. The soldier, or the state much of whose policy depends upon organized force, cannot but resent the implication that he or it is unable or unwilling to meet force with force. The life of soldiers and of armies is their spirit, and that spirit receives a serious wound when it seems — even superficially — to recoil before a threat; while with the weakening of the military body falls an element of political strength which has no analogue in Great Britain or the United States, the chief military power of which must lie ever in navies, never an aggressive factor such as armies have been.

Now, the United States has made an announcement that she will support by force a policy which may bring her into collision with states of military antecedents, indisposed by their interests to acquiesce in our position, and still less willing to accept it under appearance of threat. What preparation is necessary in case such a one is as determined to fight against our demands as we to fight for them?

Preparation for war, rightly understood, falls under two heads, — preparation and preparedness. The one is a question mainly of material, and is constant in its action. The second involves an idea of completeness. When, at a particular moment, preparations are completed, one is prepared — not otherwise. There may have been made a great deal of very necessary preparation for war without being prepared. Every constituent of preparation may be behindhand, or some elements may be perfectly ready, while others are not. In neither case can a state be said to be prepared.

In the matter of preparation for war, one clear idea should be absorbed first by every one who, recognizing that war is still a possibility, desires to see his country ready. This idea is that, however defensive in origin or in political character a war may be, the

assumption of a simple defensive in war is
ruin. War, once declared, must be waged
offensively, aggressively. The enemy must not
be fended off, but smitten down. You may
then spare him every exaction, relinquish every
gain; but till down he must be struck inces-
santly and remorselessly.

Preparation, like most other things, is a
question both of kind and of degree, of quality
and of quantity. As regards degree, the
general lines upon which it is determined
have been indicated broadly in the preceding
part of this article. The measure of degree
is the estimated force which the strongest
probable enemy can bring against you, allow-
ance being made for clear drawbacks upon
his total force, imposed by his own embarrassments and responsibilities in other parts of
the world. The calculation is partly military,
partly political, the latter, however, being the
dominant factor in the premises.

In kind, preparation is twofold, — defensive
and offensive. The former exists chiefly for
the sake of the latter, in order that offence,
the determining factor in war, may put forth
its full power, unhampered by concern for the

13

protection of the national interests or for its own resources. In naval war, coast defence is the defensive factor, the navy the offensive. Coast defence, when adequate, assures the naval commander-in-chief that his base of operations — the dock-yards and coal depots — is secure. It also relieves him and his government, by the protection afforded to the chief commercial centres, from the necessity of considering them, and so leaves the offensive arm perfectly free.

Coast defence implies coast attack. To what attacks are coasts liable? Two, principally, — blockade and bombardment. The latter, being the more difficult, includes the former, as the greater does the lesser. A fleet that can bombard can still more easily blockade. Against bombardment the necessary precaution is gun-fire, of such power and range that a fleet cannot lie within bombarding distance. This condition is obtained, where surroundings permit, by advancing the line of guns so far from the city involved that bombarding distance can be reached only by coming under their fire. But it has been demonstrated, and is accepted, that, owing to

their rapidity of movement, — like a flock of
birds on the wing, — a fleet of ships can,
without disabling loss, pass by guns before
which they could not lie. Hence arises the
necessity of arresting or delaying their progress by blocking channels, which in modern
practice is done by lines of torpedoes. The
mere moral effect of the latter is a deterrent
to a dash past, — by which, if successful, a
fleet reaches the rear of the defences, and
appears immediately before the city, which
then lies at its mercy.

Coast defence, then, implies gun-power and
torpedo lines placed as described. Be it said
in passing that only places of decisive importance, commercially or militarily, need such
defences. Modern fleets cannot afford to
waste ammunition in bombarding unimportant
towns, — at least when so far from their own
base as they would be on our coast. It is
not so much a question of money as of frit-
tering their fighting strength. It would not
pay.

Even coast defence, however, although essentially passive, should have an element of
offensive force, local in character, distinct from

the offensive navy, of which nevertheless it forms a part. To take the offensive against a floating force it must itself be afloat — naval. This offensive element of coast defence is to be found in the torpedo-boat, in its various developments. It must be kept distinct in idea from the sea-going fleet, although it is, of course, possible that the two may act in concert. The war very well may take such a turn that the sea-going navy will find its best preparation for initiating an offensive movement to be by concentrating in a principal seaport. Failing such a contingency, however, and in and for coast defence in its narrower sense, there should be a local flotilla of small torpedo-vessels, which by their activity should make life a burden to an outside enemy. A distinguished British admiral, now dead, has said that he believed half the captains of a blockading fleet would break down — "go crazy" were the words repeated to me — under the strain of modern conditions. The expression, of course, was intended simply to convey a sense of the immensity of suspense to be endured. In such a flotilla, owing to the smallness of its com-

ponents, and to the simplicity of their organization and functions, is to be found the best
sphere for naval volunteers; the duties could
be learned with comparative ease, and the
whole system is susceptible of rapid development. Be it remembered, however, that it is
essentially defensive, only incidentally offensive, in character.

Such are the main elements of coast defence
— guns, lines of torpedoes, torpedo-boats. Of
these none can be extemporized, with the
possible exception of the last, and that would
be only a makeshift. To go into details
would exceed the limits of an article, — require a brief treatise. Suffice it to say, without
the first two, coast cities are open to bombardment; without the last, they can be blockaded
freely, unless relieved by the sea-going navy.
Bombardment and blockade are recognized
modes of warfare, subject only to reasonable
notification, — a concession rather to humanity
and equity than to strict law. Bombardment
and blockade directed against great national
centres, in the close and complicated network of national and commercial interests
as they exist in modern times, strike not

only the point affected, but every corner of the land.

The offensive in naval war, as has been said, is the function of the sea-going navy — of the battle-ships, and of the cruisers of various sizes and purposes, including sea-going torpedo-vessels capable of accompanying a fleet, without impeding its movements by their loss of speed or unseaworthiness. Seaworthiness, and reasonable speed under all weather conditions, are qualities necessary to every constituent of a fleet; but, over and above these, the backbone and real power of any navy are the vessels which, by due proportion of defensive and offensive powers, are capable of taking and giving hard knocks. All others are but subservient to these, and exist only for them.

What is that strength to be? Ships answering to this description are the *kind* which make naval strength; what is to be its *degree?* What their number? The answer — a broad formula — is that it must be great enough to take the sea, and to fight, with reasonable chances of success, the largest force likely to be brought against it, as shown by calculations which have been indicated previously. Being, as we claim, and as our past history justifies us in claiming, a nation indisposed to aggression, unwilling to extend our possessions or our interests by war, the measure of strength we set ourselves depends, necessarily, not upon our projects of aggrandizement, but upon the disposition of others to thwart what we consider our reasonable policy, which they may not so consider. When they resist, what force can they bring against us? That force must be naval; we have no exposed point upon which land operations, decisive in character, can be directed. This is the kind of the hostile force to be apprehended. What may its size be? There is the measure of our needed strength. The calculation may be intricate, the conclusion only approximate and probable, but it is the nearest reply we can reach. So many ships of such and such sizes, so many guns, so much ammunition — in short, so much naval material.

In the material provisions that have been summarized under the two chief heads of defence and offence — in coast defence under its three principal requirements, guns, lines of stationary torpedoes, and torpedo-boats, and in

a navy able to keep the sea in the presence of
a probable enemy — consist what may be called
most accurately preparations for war. In so
far as the United States is short in them, she is
at the mercy of an enemy whose naval strength
is greater than that of her own available navy.
If her navy cannot keep the enemy off the
coast, blockade at least is possible. If, in addition, there are no harbor torpedo-boats, blockade
is easy. If, further, guns and torpedo lines are
deficient, bombardment comes within the range
of possibility, and may reach even the point of
entire feasibility. There will be no time for
preparation after war begins.

It is not in the preparation of material that
states generally fall most short of being ready
for war at brief notice; for such preparation is
chiefly a question of money and of manufacture, — not so much of preservation after creation. If money enough is forthcoming, a
moderate degree of foresight can insure that
the amount of material deemed necessary shall
be on hand at a given future moment; and a
similar condition can be maintained steadily.
Losses by deterioration or expenditure, or
demand for further increase if such appear

desirable, can all be forecast with reasonable calculations, and requirements thence arising can be made good. This is comparatively easy, because mere material, once wrought into shape for war, does not deteriorate from its utility to the nation because not used immediately. It can be stored and cared for at a relatively small expense, and with proper oversight will remain just as good and just as ready for use as at its first production. There are certain deductions, a certain percentage of impairment to be allowed for, but the general statement holds.

A very different question is confronted in the problem how to be ready at equally short notice to use this material, — to provide in sufficient numbers, upon a sudden call, the living agents, without whom the material is worthless. Such men in our day must be especially trained; and not only so, but while training once acquired will not be forgot wholly — stays by a man for a certain time — it nevertheless tends constantly to drop off from him. Like all habits, it requires continued practice. Moreover, it takes quite a long time to form, in a new recruit, not merely familiarity with the use of a particular weapon, but also the habit and working of the military organization of which he is an individual member. It is not enough that he learn just that one part of the whole machinery which falls to him to handle; he must be acquainted with the mutual relations of the other parts to his own and to the whole, at least in great measure. Such knowledge is essential even to the full and intelligent discharge of his own duty, not to speak of the fact that in battle every man should be ready to supply the place of another of his own class and grade who has been disabled. Unless this be so, the ship will be very far short of her best efficiency.

Now, to possess such proficiency in the handling of naval material for war, and in playing an intelligent part in the general functioning of a ship in action, much time is required. Time is required to obtain it, further time is needed in order to retain it; and such time, be it more or less, is time lost for other purposes, — lost both to the individual and to the community. When you have your thoroughly efficient man-of-war's man, you cannot store him as you do your guns and ammunition, or lay him up as you may your ships, without his deteriorating at a rate to which material presents no parallel. On the other hand, if he be retained, voluntarily or otherwise, in the naval service, there ensues the economical loss — the loss of productive power — which constitutes the great argument against large standing armies and enforced military service, advanced by those to whom the productive energies of a country outweigh all other considerations.

It is this difficulty which is felt most by those responsible for the military readiness of European states, and which therefore has engaged their most anxious attention. The providing of material of war is an onerous money question; but it is simple, and has some compensation for the expense in the resulting employment of labor for its production. It is quite another matter to have ready the number of men needed, — to train them, and to keep them so trained as to be available immediately.

The solution is sought in a tax upon time — upon the time of the nation, economically lost to production, and upon the time of the individual, lost out of his life. Like other taxes, the tendency on all sides is to reduce this as far as possible, — to compromise between ideal proficiency for probable contingencies, and the actual demands of the existing and usual conditions of peace. Although inevitable, the compromise is unsatisfactory, and yields but partial results in either direction. The economist still deplores and resists the loss of producers, — the military authorities insist that the country is short of its necessary force. To obviate the difficulty as far as possible, to meet both of the opposing demands, resort is had to the system of reserves, into which men pass after serving in the active force for a period, which is reduced to, and often below, the shortest compatible with instruction in their duties, and with the maintenance of the active forces at a fixed minimum. This instruction acquired, the recipient passes into the reserve, leaves the life of the soldier or seaman for that of the citizen, devoting a comparatively brief time in every year to brushing up the knowledge formerly acquired. Such a system, under some form, is found in services both voluntary and compulsory.

It is scarcely necessary to say that such a method would never be considered satisfactory in any of the occupations of ordinary life. A man who learns his profession or trade, but never practises it, will not long be considered fit for employment. No kind of practical preparation, in the way of systematic instruction, equals the practical knowledge imbibed in the common course of life. This is just as true of the military professions — the naval especially — as it is of civil callings; perhaps even more so, because the former are a more unnatural, and therefore, when attained, a more highly specialized, form of human activity. For the very reason that war is in the main an evil, an unnatural state, but yet at times unavoidable, the demands upon warriors, when average men, are exceptionally exacting.

Preparedness for naval war therefore consists not so much in the building of ships and guns as it does in the possession of trained men, in adequate numbers, fit to go on board at once and use the material, the provision of which is merely one of the essential preparations for war. The word "fit" includes fairly all that detail of organization commonly called mobilization, by which the movements of the individual men are combined and directed. But mobilization, although the subjects of it are men, is itself a piece of mental machinery. Once devised, it may be susceptible of improvement, but it will not become inefficient because filed away in a pigeon-hole, any more than guns and projectiles become worthless by being stored in their parks or magazines. Take care of the pence and the pounds will take care of themselves. Provide your fit men, — fit by their familiarity not only with special instruments, but with a manner of life, — and your mobilization is reduced to a slip of paper telling each one where he is to go. He will get there.

That a navy, especially a large navy, can be kept fully manned in peace — manned up to the requirements of war — must be dismissed as impracticable. If greatly superior to a probable enemy, it will be unnecessary; if more nearly equal, then the aim can only be to be superior in the number of men immediately available, and fit according to the standard of fitness here generalized. The place of a reserve in any system of preparation for war must be admitted, because inevitable. The question of the proportion and character of the reserve, relatively to the active force of peace, is the

crux of the matter. This is essentially the
question between long-service and short-service
systems. With long service the reserves will
be 'fewer, and for the first few years of retirement much more efficient, for they have acquired, not knowledge only, but a habit of life.
With short service, more men are shoved
through the mill of the training-school. Consequently they pass more rapidly into the
reserve, are less efficient when they get there,
and lose more rapidly, because they have
acquired less thoroughly; on the other hand,
they will be decidedly more numerous, on paper
at least, than the entire trained force of a
long-service system. The pessimists on either
side will expound the dangers — the one, of
short numbers ; the others, of inadequate
training.

Long service must be logically the desire,
and the result, of voluntary systems of recruit-
ing the strength of a military force. Where
enrolment is a matter of individual choice,
there is a better chance of entrance resulting
in the adoption of the life as a calling to be
followed ; and this disposition can be encouraged by the offering of suitable inducements.

Where service is compulsory, that fact alone tends to make it abhorrent, and voluntary persistence, after time has been served, rare. But, on the other hand, as the necessity for numbers in war is as real as the necessity of fitness, a body where long service and small reserves obtain should in peace be more numerous than one where the reserves are larger. To long service and small reserves a large standing force is the natural corollary. It may be added that it is more consonant to the necessities of warfare, and more consistent with the idea of the word " reserve," as elsewhere used in war. The reserve in battle is that portion of the force which is withheld from engagement, awaiting the unforeseen developments of the fight ; but no general would think of carrying on a pitched battle with the smaller part of his force, keeping the larger part in reserve. Rapid concentration of effort, anticipating that of the enemy, is the ideal of tactics and of strategy, — of the battle-field and of the campaign. It is that, likewise, of the science of mobilization, in its modern development. The reserve is but the margin of safety, to compensate for defects in conception or execution, to which all enterprises are liable; and it may be added that it is as applicable to the material force — the ships, guns, etc. — as it is to the men.

The United States, like Great Britain, depends wholly upon voluntary enlistments; and both nations, with unconscious logic, have laid great stress upon continuous service, and comparatively little upon reserves. When seamen have served the period which entitles them to the rewards of continuous service, without further enlistment, they are, though still in the prime of life, approaching the period when fitness, in the private seaman or soldier, depends upon ingrained habit — perfect practical familiarity with the life which has been their one calling — rather than upon that elastic vigor which is the privilege of youth. Should they elect to continue in the service, there still remain some years in which they are an invaluable leaven, by character and tradition. If they depart, they are for a few years a reserve for war — if they choose to come forward ; but it is manifest that such a reserve can be but small, when compared with a system which in three or five years passes men through the

14

active force into the reserve. The latter, however, is far less valuable, man for man. Of
course, a reserve which has not even three
years' service is less valuable still.

The United States is to all intents an insular
power, like Great Britain. We have but two
land frontiers, Canada and Mexico. The latter
is hopelessly inferior to us in all the elements
of military strength. As regards Canada,
Great Britain maintains a standing army; but,
like our own, its numbers indicate clearly that
aggression will never be her policy, except in
those distant regions whither the great armies
of the world cannot act against her, unless they
first wrench from her the control of the sea.
No modern state has long maintained a supremacy by land and by sea, — one or the other
has been held from time to time by this or that
country, but not both. Great Britain wisely
has chosen naval power; and, independent of
her reluctance to break with the United States
for other reasons, she certainly would regret to
devote to the invasion of a nation of seventy
millions the small disposable force which she
maintains in excess of the constant requirements of her colonial interests. We are, it

may be repeated, an insular power, dependent therefore upon a navy.

Durable naval power, besides, depends ultimately upon extensive commercial relations; consequently, and especially in an insular state, it is rarely aggressive, in the military sense. Its instincts are naturally for peace, because it has so much at stake outside its shores. Historically, this has been the case with the conspicuous example of sea power, Great Britain, since she became such; and it increasingly tends to be so. It is also our own case, and to a yet greater degree, because, with an immense compact territory, there has not been the disposition to external effort which has carried the British flag all over the globe, seeking to earn by foreign commerce and distant settlement that abundance of resource which to us has been the free gift of nature — or of Providence. By her very success, however, Great Britain, in the vast increase and dispersion of her external interests, has given hostages to fortune, which for mere defence impose upon her a great navy. Our career has been different, our conditions now are not identical, yet our geographical position and political convic-

tions have created for us also external interests
and external responsibilities, which are likewise
our hostages to fortune.   It is not necessary to
roam afar in search of adventures; popular
feeling and the deliberate judgment of statesmen alike have asserted that, from conditions
we neither made nor control, interests beyond
the sea exist, have sprung up of themselves,
which demand protection.   " Beyond the sea "
— that means a navy.   Of invasion, in any real
sense of the word, we run no risk, and if we
did, it must be by sea; and there, at sea, must
be met primarily, and ought to be met decisively, any attempt at invasion of our interests,
either in distant lands, or at home by blockade
or by bombardment.   Yet the force of men in
the navy is smaller, by more than half, than
that in the army.

The necessary complement of those admirable measures which have been employed now
for over a decade in the creation of naval material is the preparation of an adequate force of
trained men to use this material when completed.   Take an entirely fresh man : a battle-
ship can be built and put in commission before
he becomes a trained man-of-war's man, and a

torpedo-boat can be built and ready for service before, to use the old sea phrase, " the hay seed is out of his hair." Further, in a voluntary service, you cannot keep your trained men as you can ·your completed ship or gun. The inevitable inference is that the standing force must be large, because you can neither create it hastily nor maintain it by compulsion. Having fixed the amount of material, — the numbers and character of the fleet, — from this follows easily the number of men necessary to man it. This aggregate force can then be distributed, upon some accepted idea, between the standing navy and the reserve. Without fixing a proportion between the two, the present writer is convinced that the reserve should be but a small percentage of the whole, and that in a small navy, as ours, relatively, long will be, this is doubly imperative; for the smaller the navy, the greater the need for constant efficiency to act promptly, and the smaller the expense of maintenance. In fact, where quantity — number — is small, quality should be all the more high. The quality of the whole is a question of *personnel* even more than of material; and the quality of the *personnel* can be maintained only by high individual fitness in the force, undiluted by dependence upon a large, only partly efficient, reserve element.

" One foot on sea and one on shore, to one thing constant never,"

will not man the fleet. It can be but an imperfect palliative, and can be absorbed effectually by the main body only in small proportions. It is in torpedo-boats for coast defence, and in commerce-destroying for deep-sea warfare, that the true sphere for naval reserves will be found; for the duties in both cases are comparatively simple, and the organization can be the same.

Every danger of a military character to which the United States is exposed can be met best outside her own territory — at sea. Preparedness for naval war — preparedness against naval attack and for naval offence — is preparedness for anything that is likely to occur.

A TWENTIETH-CENTURY OUTLOOK.

A TWENTIETH–CENTURY OUTLOOK.

May, 1897.

FINALITY, the close of a life, of a relation-
ship, of an era, even though this be a purely
artificial creation of human arrangement, in all
cases appeals powerfully to the imagination, and
especially to that of a generation self-conscious
as ours, a generation which has coined for itself
the phrase *fin de siècle* to express its belief, however superficial and mistaken, that it knows its
own exponents and its own tendencies; that,
amid the din of its own progress sounding in
its ears, it knows not only whence it comes but
whither it goes. The nineteenth century is
about to die, only to rise again in the twentieth.
Whence did it come? How far has it gone?
Whither is it going?

A full reply to such queries would presume an
abridged universal history of the expiring cen-

tury such as a magazine article, or series of articles, could not contemplate for a moment. The scope proposed to himself by the present writer, itself almost unmanageable within the necessary limits, looks not to the internal conditions of states, to those economical and social tendencies which occupy so large a part of contemporary attention, seeming to many the sole subjects that deserve attention, and that from the most purely material and fleshly point of view. Important as these things are, it may be affirmed at least that they are not everything; and that, great as has been the material progress of the century, the changes in international relations and relative importance, not merely in states of the European family, but among the peoples of the world at large, have been no less striking. It is from this direction that the writer wishes to approach his subject, which, if applied to any particular country, might be said to be that of its external relations; but which, in the broader view that it will be sought to attain, regards rather the general future of the world as indicated by movements already begun and in progress, as well as by tendencies now dimly discernible, which, if not counteracted, are pregnant of further momentous shifting of the political balances, profoundly affecting the welfare of mankind.

It appears a convenient, though doubtless very rough, way of prefacing this subject to say that the huge colonizing movements of the eighteenth century were brought to a pause by the American Revolution, which deprived Great Britain of her richest colonies, succeeded, as that almost immediately was, by the French Revolution and the devastating wars of the republic and of Napoleon, which forced the attention of Europe to withdraw from external allurements and to concentrate upon its own internal affairs. The purchase of Louisiana by the United States at the opening of the current century empha-sized this conclusion; for it practically elimi-nated the continent of North America from the catalogue of wild territories available for foreign settlement. Within a decade this was succeeded by the revolt of the Spanish colo-nies, followed later by the pronouncements of President Monroe and of Mr. Canning, which assured their independence by preventing Euro-pean interference. The firmness with which the position of the former statesman has been maintained ever since by the great body of the people of the United States, and the developments his doctrine afterwards received, have removed the Spanish-American countries equally from all probable chance of further European colonization, in the political sense of the word.

Thus the century opened. Men's energies still sought scope beyond the sea, doubtless; not, however, in the main, for the founding of new colonies, but for utilizing ground already in political occupation. Even this, however, was subsidiary. The great work of the nineteenth century, from nearly its beginning to nearly its close, has been in the recognition and study of the forces of nature, and the application of them to the purposes of mechanical and economical advance. The means thus placed in men's hands, so startling when first invented, so familiar for the most part to us now, were devoted necessarily, first, to the development of the resources of each country. Everywhere there was a fresh field; for hitherto it had been nowhere possible to man fully to utilize the gifts of nature. Energies everywhere turned inward, for there, in every region, was more than enough to do. Naturally, there-fore, such a period has been in the main one of peace. There have been great wars, certainly; but, nevertheless, external peace has been the general characteristic of that period of develop-ment, during which men have been occupied in revolutionizing the face of their own coun-tries by means of the new powers at their disposal.

All such phases pass, however, as does every human thing. Increase of production — the idol of the economist — sought fresh markets, as might have been predicted. The increase of home consumption, through increased ease of living, increased wealth, increased population, did not keep up with the increase of forth-putting and the facility of distribution afforded by steam. In the middle of the century China and Japan were forced out of the seclusion of ages, and were compelled, for commercial pur-poses at least, to enter into relations with the European communities, to buy and to sell with them. Serious attempts, on any extensive scale, to acquire new political possessions abroad largely ceased. Commerce only sought new footholds, sure that, given the inch, she in the end would have the ell.   Moreover, the growth of the United States in population and resources, and the development of the British Australian colonies, contributed to meet the demand, of which the opening of China and Japan was only a single indication.   That opening, therefore, was rather an incident of the general industrial development which followed upon the improvement of mechanical processes and the multiplication of communications.

Thus the century passed its meridian, and began to decline towards its close.   There were wars and there were rumors of wars in the countries of European civilization.   Dynasties rose and fell, and nations shifted their places in the scale of political importance, as old-time boys in school went up and down; but, withal, the main characteristic abode, and has become more and more the dominant prepossession of the statesmen who reached their prime at or soon after the times when the century itself culminated.   The maintenance of a *status quo*, for purely utilitarian reasons of an economical character, has gradually become an ideal — the *quieta non movere* of Sir Robert Walpole.   The ideal is respectable, certainly; in view of the concert of the powers, in the interest of their own repose, to coerce Greece and the Cretans, we may perhaps refrain from calling it noble. The question remains, how long can it continue respectable in the sense of being practicable of realization, — a rational possibility, not an idle dream? Many are now found to say — and among them some of the most bitter of the advocates of universal peace, who are among the bitterest of modern disputants — that when the Czar Nicholas proposed to move the quiet things, half a century ago, and to reconstruct the political map of southeastern Europe in the interest of well-founded quiet, it was he that showed the idealism of rational statesmanship, — the only truly practical statesmanship, — while the defenders of the *status quo* evinced the crude instincts of the mere time-serving politician. That the latter did not insure quiet, even the quiet of desolation, in those unhappy regions, we have yearly evidence. How far is it now a practicable object, among the nations of the European family, to continue indefinitely the present realization of peace and plenty, — in themselves good things, but which are advocated largely on the ground that man lives by bread alone, — in view of the changed conditions of the world which the departing nineteenth century leaves with us as its bequest? Is the outlook such that our present civilization, with its benefits, is most likely to be insured by universal disarmament, the clamor for which rises ominously — the word is used advisedly — among our latter-day cries? None shares more heartily than the writer the aspiration for the day when nations shall beat their swords into ploughshares and their spears into pruning-hooks; but is European civilization, including America, so situated that it can afford to relax into an artificial peace, resting not upon the working of national consciences, as questions arise, but upon a Permanent Tribunal, — an external, if self-imposed authority, — the realization in modern policy of the ideal of the mediæval Papacy?

The outlook — the signs of the times, what are they? It is not given to human vision, peering into the future, to see more than as through a glass, darkly; men as trees walking, one cannot say certainly whither. Yet signs may be noted even if they cannot be fully or precisely interpreted; and among them I should

certainly say is to be observed the general outward impulse of all the civilized nations of
the first order of greatness — except our own.
Bound and swathed in the traditions of our
own eighteenth century, when we were as truly
external to the European world as we are now a
part of it, we, under the specious plea of peace
and plenty — fulness of bread — hug an ideal
of isolation, and refuse to recognize the solidarity of interest with which the world of
European civilization must not only look forward to, but go out to meet, the future that,
whether near or remote, seems to await it. I
say *we* do so; I should more surely express my
thought by saying that the outward impulse
already is in the majority of the nation, as
shown when particular occasions arouse their
attention, but that it is as yet retarded, and
may be retarded perilously long, by those
whose views of national policy are governed
by maxims framed in the infancy of the
Republic.

This outward impulse of the European
nations, resumed on a large scale after nearly
a century of intermission, is not a mere sudden appearance, sporadic, and unrelated to the

past. The signs of its coming, though un-
noted, were visible soon after the century
reached its half-way stage, as was also its
great correlative, equally unappreciated then,
though obvious enough now, the stirring of
the nations of Oriental civilization. It is a
curious reminiscence of my own that when in
Yokohama, Japan, in 1868, I was asked to
translate a Spanish letter from Honolulu,
relative to a ship-load of Japanese coolies to
be imported into Hawaii. I knew the person
engaged to go as physician to the ship, and,
unless my memory greatly deceives me, he
sailed in this employment while I was still in
the port. Similarly, when my service on the
station was ended, I went from Yokohama to
Hong-kong, prior to returning home by way
of Suez. Among my fellow-passengers was
an ex-Confederate naval officer, whose business was to negotiate for an immigration of
Chinese into, I think, the Southern States —
in momentary despair, perhaps, of black labor
— but certainly into the United States. We
all know what has come in our own country
of undertakings which then had attracted little
attention.

It is odd to watch the unconscious, resist-less movements of nations, and at the same time read the crushing characterization by our teachers of the press of those who, by per-sonal characteristics or by accident, happen to be thrust into the position of leaders, when at the most they only guide to the least harm forces which can no more be resisted perma-nently than can gravitation. Such would have been the rôle of Nicholas, guiding to a timely end the irresistible course of events in the Balkans, which his opponents sought to with-stand, but succeeded only in prolonging and aggravating. He is honored now by those who see folly in the imperial aspirations of Mr. Joseph Chamberlain, and piracy in Mr. Cecil Rhodes; yet, after all, in his day, what right had he, by the code of strict construc-tionists of national legal rights, to put Turkey to death because she was sick? Was not Turkey in occupation? Had she not, by strict law, a right to her possessions, and to live; yea, and to administer what she con-sidered justice to those who were legally her subjects? But men are too apt to forget that law is the servant of equity, and that while the world is in its present stage of development equity which cannot be had by law must be had by force, upon which ultimately law rests, not for its sanction, but for its efficacy.

We have been familiar latterly with the term " buffer states ; " the pleasant function discharged by Siam between Great Britain and France. Though not strictly analogous, the term conveys an idea of the relations that have hitherto obtained between Eastern and Western civilizations. They have existed apart, each a world of itself; but they are approaching not only in geographical propinquity, a recognized source of danger, but, what is more important, in common ideas of material advantage, without a corresponding sympathy in spiritual ideas. It is not merely that the two are in different stages of development from a common source, as are Russia and Great Britain. They are running as yet on wholly different lines, springing from conceptions radically different. To bring them into correspondence in that, the most important realm of ideas, there is needed on the one side — or on the other — not growth, but conversion. However far it has wandered, and however short of its pattern it has come, the civilization of modern Europe grew up under the shadow of the Cross, and what is best in it still breathes the spirit of the Crucified. It is to be feared that Eastern thinkers consider it rather an advantage than a detriment that they are appropriating the material progress of Europe unfettered by Christian traditions, — as agnostic countries. But, for the present at least, agnosticism with Christian ages behind it is a very different thing from agnosticism which has never known Christianity.

What will be in the future the dominant spiritual ideas of those nations which hitherto have been known as Christian, is scarcely a question of the twentieth century. Whatever variations of faith, in direction or in degree, the close of that century may show, it is not probable that so short a period will reveal the full change of standards and of practice which necessarily must follow ultimately upon a radical change of belief. That the impress of Christianity will remain throughout the coming century is reasonably as certain as that it took centuries of nominal faith to lift Christian standards and practice even to the point they now have reached. Decline, as well as rise, must be gradual; and gradual likewise, granting the utmost possible spread of Christian beliefs among them, will be the approximation of the Eastern nations, as nations, to the principles which powerfully modify, though they cannot control wholly even now, the merely natural impulses of Western peoples. And if, as many now say, faith has departed from among ourselves, and still more will depart in the coming years; if we have no higher sanction to propose for self-restraint and righteousness than enlightened self-interest and the absurdity of war, war — violence — will be absurd just so long as the balance of interest is on that side, and no longer. Those who want will take, if they can, not merely from motives of high policy and as legal opportunity offers, but for the simple reasons that they have not, that they desire, and that they are able. The European world has known that stage already; it has escaped from it only partially by the gradual hallowing of public opinion and its growing weight in the political scale. The Eastern world knows not the same motives, but it is rapidly appreciating the material advantages and the political traditions which have united to confer power upon the West; and with the appreciation desire has arisen.

Coincident with the long pause which the French Revolution imposed upon the process of external colonial expansion which was so marked a feature of the eighteenth century, there occurred another singular manifestation of national energies, in the creation of the great standing armies of modern days, themselves the outcome of the *levée en masse*, and of the general conscription, which the Revolution bequeathed to us along with its expositions of the Rights of Man. Beginning with the birth of the century, perfected during its continuance, its close finds them in full maturity and power, with a development in numbers, in reserve force, in organization, and in material for war, over which the economist perpetually wails, whose existence he denounces, and whose abolition he demands. As freedom has grown and strengthened, so have they grown and strengthened. Is this singular product of a century whose gains for political liberty are undeniable, a mere gross perversion of human activities, as is so confidently claimed on many

sides? or is there possibly in it also a sign of
the times to come, to be studied in connection with other signs, some of which we have
noted ?

What has been the effect of these great
armies ? Manifold, doubtless. On the economical side there is the diminution of production,
the tax upon men's time and lives, the disadvantages or evils so dinned daily into our ears
that there is no need of repeating them here.
But is there nothing to the credit side of the
account, even perhaps a balance in their favor?
Is it nothing, in an age when authority is
weakening and restraints are loosening, that
the youth of a nation passes through a school
in which order, obedience, and reverence are
learned, where the body is systematically developed, where ideals of self-surrender, of courage,
of manhood, are inculcated, necessarily, because
fundamental conditions of military success?
Is it nothing that masses of youths out of the
fields and the streets are brought together,
mingled with others of higher intellectual antecedents, taught to work and to act together,
mind in contact with mind, and carrying
back into civil life that respect for constituted

authority which is urgently needed in these days when lawlessness is erected into a religion? It is a suggestive lesson to watch the expression and movements of a number of rustic conscripts undergoing their first drills, and to contrast them with the finished result as seen in the faces and bearing of the soldiers that throng the streets. A military training is not the worst preparation for an active life, any more than the years spent at college are time lost, as another school of utilitarians insists. Is it nothing that wars are less frequent, peace better secured, by the mutual respect of nations for each other's strength; and that, when a convulsion does come, it passes rapidly, leaving the ordinary course of events to resume sooner, and therefore more easily? War now not only occurs more rarely, but has rather the character of an occasional excess, from which recovery is easy. A century or more ago it was a chronic disease. And withal, the military spirit, the preparedness — not merely the willingness, which is a different thing — to fight in a good cause, which is a distinct good, is more widely diffused and more thoroughly possessed than ever it was when the soldier was merely the paid man. It is the nations now that are in arms, and not simply the servants of the king.

In forecasting the future, then, it is upon these particular signs of the times that I dwell: the arrest of the forward impulse towards political colonization which coincided with the decade immediately preceding the French Revolution; the absorption of the European nations, for the following quarter of a century, with the universal wars, involving questions chiefly political and European; the beginning of the great era of coal and iron, of mechanical and industrial development, which succeeded the peace, and during which it was not aggressive colonization, but the development of colonies already held and of new commercial centres, notably in China and Japan, that was the most prominent feature; finally, we have, resumed at the end of the century, the forward movement of political colonization by the mother countries, powerfully incited thereto, doubtless, by the citizens of the old colonies in different parts of the world. The restlessness of Australia and the Cape Colony has doubtless counted for much in British advances in those regions. Contemporary with all these movements, from the first to the last, has been the development of great standing armies, or rather of armed nations, in Europe; and, lastly, the stirring of the East, its entrance into the field of Western interests, not merely as a passive something to be impinged upon, but with a vitality of its own, formless yet, but significant, inasmuch as where before there was torpor, if not death, now there is indisputable movement and life. Never again, probably, can there of it be said,

> "It heard the legions thunder past,
> Then plunged in thought again."

Of this the astonishing development of Japan is the most obvious evidence; but in India, though there be no probability of the old mutinies reviving, there are signs enough of the awaking of political intelligence, restlessness under foreign subjection, however beneficent, desire for greater play for its own individualities; a movement which, because intellectual and appreciative of the advantages of Western material and political civilization, is less immediately threatening than the former revolt, but much more ominous of great future changes.

Of China we know less; but many observers testify to the immense latent force of the Chinese character. It has shown itself hitherto chiefly in the strength with which it has adhered to stereotyped tradition. But stereotyped traditions have been overthrown already more than once even in this unprogressive people, whose conservatism, due largely to ignorance of better conditions existing in other lands, is closely allied also to the unusual staying powers of the race, to the persistence of purpose, the endurance, and the vitality characteristic of its units. To ambition for individual material improvement they are not insensible. The collapse of the Chinese organization in all its branches during the late war with Japan, though greater than was expected, was not unforeseen. It has not altered the fact that the raw material so miserably utilized is, in point of strength, of the best; that it is abundant, racially homogeneous, and is multiplying rapidly. Nor, with the recent resuscitation of the Turkish army before men's eyes, can it be thought unlikely that the Chinese may yet obtain the organization by which alone potential force receives adequate military development, the most easily conferred because the simplest in conception. The Japanese have shown great capacity, but they met little resistance; and it is easier by far to move and to control an island kingdom of forty millions than a vast continental territory containing near tenfold that number of inhabitants. Comparative slowness of evolution may be predicated, but that which for so long has kept China one, amid many diversities, may be counted upon in the future to insure a substantial unity of impulse which, combined with its mass, will give tremendous import to any movement common to the whole.

To assert that a few selected characteristics, such as the above, summarize the entire tendency of a century of teeming human life, and stand alone among the signs that are chiefly to be considered in looking to the future, would be to take an untenable position. It may be said safely, however, that these factors, because the future to which they point is more remote, are less regarded than others which are less important; and further, that those among them which mark our own day are also the factors whose very existence is specially resented, criticised, and condemned by that school of political thought which assumes for itself the title of economical, which attained its maturity, and still lives, amid the ideas of that stage of industrial progress coincident with the middle of the century, and which sees all things from the point of view of production and of internal development. Powerfully exerted throughout the world, nowhere is the influence of this school so unchecked and so injurious as in the United States, because, having no near neighbors to compete with us in point of power, military necessities have been to us not imminent, so that, like all distant dangers, they have received little regard; and also because, with our great resources only partially developed, the instinct to external activities has remained dormant. At the same period and from the same causes that the European world turned its eyes inward from the seaboard, instead of outward, the people of the United States were similarly diverted from the external activities in which at the beginning of the century they had their wealth. This tendency, emphasized on the political side by the civil war, was reinforced and has been prolonged by well-known natural conditions. A territory much larger, far less redeemed from its original wildness, and with perhaps even ampler proportionate resources than the continent of Europe, contained a much smaller number of inhabitants. Hence, despite an immense immigration, we have lagged far behind in the work of completing our internal development, and for that reason have not yet felt the outward impulse that now markedly characterizes the European peoples. That we stand far apart from the general movement of our race calls of itself for consideration.

For the reasons mentioned it has been an easy but a short-sighted policy, wherever it has been found among statesmen or among journalists, to fasten attention purely on internal and economical questions, and to reject, if not to resent, propositions looking towards the organization and maintenance of military force, or contemplating the extension of our national influence beyond our own borders, on the plea that we have enough to do at home, — forgetful that no nation, as no man, can live to itself or die to itself. It is a policy in which we are

behind our predecessors of two generations
ago, men who had not felt the deadening influence of merely economical ideas, because
they reached manhood before these attained
the preponderance they achieved under politi-
cians of the Manchester school; a preponderance which they still retain because the youths
of that time, who grew up under them, have
not yet quite passed off the stage. It is the
lot of each generation, salutary no doubt, to be
ruled by men whose ideas are essentially those
of a former day. Breaches of continuity in
national action are thus moderated or avoided;
but, on the other hand, the tendency of such a
condition is to blind men to the spirit of the
existing generation, because its rulers have the
tone of their own past, and direct affairs in
accordance with it. On the very day of this
writing there appears in an American journal
a slashing contrast between the action of Lord
Salisbury in the Cretan business and the spir-
ited letter of Mr. Gladstone upon the failure of
the Concert. As a matter of fact, however, both
those British statesmen, while belonging to
parties traditionally opposed, are imbued above
all with the ideas of the middle of the century,

and, governed by them, consider the disturbance of quiet the greatest of all evils. It is difficult to believe that if Mr. Gladstone were now in his prime, and in power, any object would possess in his eyes an importance at all comparable to that of keeping the peace. He would feel for the Greeks, doubtless, as Lord Salisbury doubtless does; but he would maintain the Concert as long as he believed that alone would avoid war. When men in sympathy with the ideas now arising among Englishmen come on the stage, we shall see a change — not before.

The same spirit has dominated in our own country ever since the civil war — a far more real "revolution" in its consequences than the struggle of the thirteen colonies against Great Britain, which in our national speech has received the name — forced our people, both North and South, to withdraw their eyes from external problems, and to concentrate heart and mind with passionate fervor upon an internal strife, in which one party was animated by the inspiring hope of independence, while before the other was exalted the noble ideal of union. That war, however, was directed, on the civil side, by men who belonged to a generation even then passing away. The influence of their own youth reverted with the return of peace, and was to be seen in the ejection — by threat of force — of the third Napoleon from Mexico, in the acquisition of Alaska, and in the negotiations for the purchase of the Danish islands and of Samana Bay. Whatever may have been the wisdom of these latter attempts, — and the writer, while sympathizing with the spirit that suggested them, questions it from a military, or rather naval, stand-point, — they are particularly interesting as indicating the survival in elderly men of the traditions accepted in their youth, but foreign to the generation then rapidly coming into power, which rejected and frustrated them.

The latter in turn is now disappearing, and its successors, coming and to come, are crowding into its places. Is there any indication of the ideas these bring with them, in their own utterances, or in the spirit of the world at large, which they must needs reflect; or, more important perhaps still, is there any indication in the conditions of the outside world itself which they should heed, and the influence of which they should admit, in modifying and shaping their policies, before these have become hardened into fixed lines, directive for many years of the future welfare of their people?

To all these questions the writer, as one of the departing generation, would answer yes; but it is to the last that his attention, possibly by constitutional bias, is more naturally directed. It appears to him that in the ebb and flow of human affairs, under those mysterious impulses the origin of which is sought by some in a personal Providence, by some in laws not yet fully understood, we stand at the opening of a period when the question is to be settled decisively, though the issue may be long delayed, whether Eastern or Western civilization is to dominate throughout the earth and to control its future. The great task now before the world of civilized Christianity, its great mission, which it must fulfil or perish, is to receive into its own bosom and raise to its own ideals those ancient and different civilizations by which it is surrounded and outnumbered, — the civilizations at the head of which stand China, India, and Japan. This, to cite the most striking of the many forms in which it is presented to us, is surely the mission which Great Britain, sword ever at hand, has been discharging towards India; but that stands not alone. The history of the present century has been that of a constant increasing pressure of our own civilization upon these older ones, till now, as we cast our eyes in any direction, there is everywhere a stirring, a rousing from sleep, drowsy for the most part, but real, unorganized as yet, but conscious that that which rudely interrupts their dream of centuries possesses over them at least two advantages, — power and material prosperity, — the things which unspiritual humanity, the world over, most craves.

What the ultimate result will be it would be vain to prophesy, — the data for a guess even are not at hand; but it is not equally impossible to note present conditions, and to suggest present considerations, which may shape proximate action, and tend to favor the preponderance of that form of civilization which we cannot but deem the most promising for the future, not of our race only, but of the world at large. We are not living in a perfect world, and we may not expect to deal with imperfect conditions by methods ideally perfect. Time and staying power must be secured for ourselves by that rude and imperfect, but not ignoble, arbiter, force, —force potential and force organized, — which so far has won, and still secures, the greatest triumphs of good in the checkered history of mankind. Our material advantages, once noted, will be recognized readily and appropriated with avidity; while the spiritual ideas which dominate our thoughts, and are weighty in their influence over action, even with those among us who do not accept historic Christianity or the ordinary creeds of Christendom, will be rejected for long. The eternal law, first that which is natural, afterwards that which is spiritual, will obtain here, as in the individual, and in the long history of our own civilization. Between the two there is an interval, in which force must be ready to redress any threatened disturbance of an equal balance between those who stand on divergent planes of thought, without common standards.

And yet more is this true if, as is commonly said, faith is failing among ourselves, if the progress of our own civilization is towards the loss of those spiritual convictions upon which it was founded, and which in early days were mighty indeed towards the overthrowing of strongholds of evil. What, in such a case, shall play the tremendous part which the Church of the Middle Ages, with all its defects and with all the shortcomings of its ministers, played amid the ruin of the Roman Empire and the flood of the barbarians? If our own civilization is becoming material only, a thing limited in hope and love to this world, I know not what we have to offer to save ourselves or others; but in either event, whether to go down finally under a flood of outside invasion, or whether to succeed, by our own living faith, in converting to our ideal civilization those who shall thus press upon us, — in either event we need time, and time can be gained only by organized material force.

Nor is this view advanced in any spirit of unfriendliness to the other ancient civilizations, whose genius admittedly has been and is foreign to our own. One who believes that God has made of one blood all nations of men who dwell on the face of the whole earth cannot but check and repress, if he ever feels, any movement of aversion to mankind outside his own race. But it is not necessary to hate Carthage in order to admit that it was well for mankind that Rome triumphed; and we at this day, and men to all time, may be thankful that a few decades after the Punic Wars the genius of Cæsar so expanded the bounds of the dominions of Rome, so extended, settled, and solidified the outworks of her civilization and polity, that when the fated day came that her power in turn should reel under the shock of conquest, with which she had remodelled the world, and she should go down herself, the time of the final fall was protracted for centuries by these exterior defences. They who began the assault as barbarians entered upon the imperial heritage no longer aliens and foreigners, but impregnated already with the best of Roman ideas, converts to Roman law and to Christian faith.

"When the course of history," says Mommsen, "turns from the miserable monotony of the political selfishness which fought its battles in the Senate House and in the streets of Rome, we may be allowed — on the threshold of an event the effects of which still at the present day influence the destinies of the world — to look round us for a moment, and to indicate the point of view under which the conquest of what is now France by the Romans, and their first contact with the inhabitants of Germany and of Great Britain, are to be regarded in connection with the general history of the world. . . . The fact that the great Celtic people were ruined by the transalpine wars of Cæsar was not the most important result of that grand enterprise, — far more momentous than the negative was the positive result. It hardly admits of a doubt that if the rule of the Senate had prolonged its semblance of life for some generations longer, the migration of the peoples, as it is called, would have occurred four hundred years sooner than it did, and would have occurred at a time when the Italian civilization had not become naturalized either in Gaul or on the Danube or in Africa and Spain. Inasmuch as Cæsar with sure glance perceived in the German tribes the rival antagonists of the Romano-Greek world, inasmuch as with firm hand he established the new system of aggressive defence down even to its details, and taught men to protect the frontiers of the empire by rivers or artificial ramparts, to colonize the nearest barbarian tribes along the frontier

with the view of warding off the more remote,
and to recruit the Roman army by enlistment
from the enemy's country, he gained for the
Hellenic-Italian culture the interval necessary
to civilize the West, just as it had already civilized the East. . . . Centuries elapsed before
men understood that Alexander had not merely
erected an ephemeral kingdom in the East, but
had carried Hellenism to Asia; centuries again
elapsed before men understood that Cæsar had
not merely conquered a new province for the
Romans, but had laid the foundation for the
Romanizing of the regions of the West. It
was only a late posterity that perceived the
meaning of those expeditions to England and
Germany, so inconsiderate in a military point
of view, and so barren of immediate result. . . .
That there is a bridge connecting the past glory
of Hellas and Rome with the prouder fabric of
modern history; that western Europe is Ro-
manic, and Germanic Europe classic; that the
names of Themistocles and Scipio have to
us a very different sound from those of Asoka
and Salmanassar; that Homer and Sophocles
are not merely like the Vedas and Kalidasa,
attractive to the literary botanist, but bloom

for us in our own garden, — all this is the work of Cæsar."

History at times reveals her foresight concrete in the action of a great individuality like Cæsar's. More often her profounder movements proceed from impulses whose origin and motives cannot be traced, although a succession of steps may be discerned and their results stated. A few names, for instance, emerge amid the obscure movements of the peoples which precipitated the outer peoples upon the Roman Empire, but, with rare exceptions, they are simply exponents, pushed forward and upward by the torrent; at the utmost guides, not controllers, of those whom they represent but do not govern. It is much the same now. The peoples of European civilization, after a period of comparative repose, are again advancing all along the line, to occupy not only the desert places of the earth, but the debatable grounds, the buffer territories, which hitherto have separated them from those ancient nations, with whom they now soon must stand face to face and border to border. But who will say that this vast general movement represents the thought, even the unconscious thought, of any one man, as Cæsar, or of any few men? To whatever cause we may assign it, whether to the simple conception of a personal Divine Monarchy that shapes our ends, or to more complicated ultimate causes, the responsibility rests upon the shoulders of no individual men. Necessity is laid upon the peoples, and they move, like the lemmings of Scandinavia; but to man, being not without understanding like the beasts that perish, it is permitted to ask, "Whither?" and "What shall be the end hereof?" Does this tend to universal peace, general disarmament, and treaties of permanent arbitration? Is it the harbinger of ready mutual understanding, of quick acceptance of, and delight in, opposing traditions and habits of life and thought? Is such quick acceptance found now where Easterns and Westerns impinge? Does contact forebode the speedy disappearance of great armies and navies, and dictate the wisdom of dispensing with that form of organized force which at present is embodied in them?

What, then, will be the actual conditions when these civilizations, of diverse origin and radically distinct, — because the evolution of racial characteristics radically different, — confront each other without the interposition of any neutral belt, by the intervention of which the contrasts, being more remote, are less apparent, and within which distinctions shade one into the other?

There will be seen, on the one hand, a vast preponderance of numbers, and those numbers, however incoherent now in mass, composed of units which in their individual capacity have in no small degree the great elements of strength whereby man prevails over man and the fittest survives. Deficient, apparently, in aptitude for political and social organization, they have failed to evolve the aggregate power and intellectual scope of which as communities they are otherwise capable. This lesson too they may learn, as they already have learned from us much that they have failed themselves to originate; but to the lack of it is chiefly due the inferiority of material development under which, as compared to ourselves, they now labor. But men do not covet less the prosperity which they themselves cannot or do not create, — a trait wherein lies the strength of communism as an aggressive social force. Communities which want and cannot have, except by force, will take by force, unless they are restrained by force ; nor will it be unprecedented in the history of the world that the flood of numbers should pour over and sweep away the barriers which intelligent foresight, like Cæsar's, may have erected against them. Still more will this be so if the barriers have ceased to be manned — forsaken or neglected by men in whom the proud combative spirit of their ancestors has given way to the cry for the abandonment of military preparation and to the decay of warlike habits.

Nevertheless, even under such conditions, — which obtained increasingly during the decline of the Roman Empire, — positions suitably chosen, frontiers suitably advanced, will do much to retard and, by gaining time, to modify the disaster to the one party, and to convert the general issue to the benefit of the world. Hence the immense importance of discerning betimes what the real value of positions is, and where occupation should betimes begin. Here, in part at least, is the significance of the great outward movement of the European nations to-day. Consciously or unconsciously, they are advancing the outposts of our civilization, and accumulating the line of defences which will permit it to survive, or at the least will insure that it shall not go down till it has leavened the character of the world for a future brighter even than its past, just as the Roman civilization inspired and exalted its Teutonic conquerors, and continues to bless them to this day.

Such is the tendency of movement in that which we in common parlance call the Old World. As the nineteenth century closes, the tide has already turned and the current is flowing strongly. It is not too soon, for vast is the work before it. Contrasted to the outside world in extent and population, the civilization of the European group of families, to which our interests and anxieties, our hopes and fears, are so largely confined, has been as an oasis in a desert. The seat and scene of the loftiest culture, of the highest intellectual activities, it is not in them so much that it has exceeded the rest of the world as in the politi-

cal development and material prosperity which
it has owed to the virile energies of its sons,
alike in commerce and in war. To these
energies the mechanical and scientific acquire-
ments of the past half-century or more have
extended means whereby prosperity has increased manifold, as have the inequalities in
material well-being existing between those within its borders and those without, who have not
had the opportunity or the wit to use the
same advantages. And along with this pre-
eminence in wealth arises the cry to disarm,
as though the race, not of Europe only, but
of the world, were already run, and the goal
of universal peace not only reached but secured. Yet are conditions such, even within
our favored borders, that we are ready to dis-
band the particular organized manifestation
of physical force which we call the police?

Despite internal jealousies and friction on
the continent of Europe, perhaps even because
of them, the solidarity of the European family
therein contained is shown in this great
common movement, the ultimate beneficence
of which is beyond all doubt, as evidenced by
the British domination in India and Egypt,

and to which the habit of arms not only contributes, but is essential. India and Egypt are at present the two most conspicuous, though they are not the sole, illustrations of benefits innumerable and lasting, which rest upon the power of the sword in the hands of enlightenment and justice. It is possible, of course, to confuse this conclusion, to obscure the real issue, by dwelling upon details of wrongs at times inflicted, of blunders often made. Any episode in the struggling progress of humanity may be thus perplexed; but looking at the broad result, it is indisputable that the vast gains to humanity made in the regions named not only once originated, but still rest, upon the exertion and continued maintenance of organized physical force.

The same general solidarity as against the outside world, which is unconsciously manifested in the general resumption of colonizing movements, receives particular conscious expression in the idea of imperial federation, which, amid the many buffets and reverses common to all successful movements, has gained such notable ground in the sentiment of the British people and of their colonists.

That immense practical difficulties have to be overcome, in order to realize the ends towards which such sentiments point, is but a common-place of human experience in all ages and countries. They give rise to the ready sneer of impossible, just as any project of extending the sphere of the United States, by annexation or otherwise, is met by the constitutional lion in the path, which the unwilling or the apprehensive is ever sure to find; yet, to use words of one who never lightly admitted impossibilities, " If a thing is necessary to be done, the more difficulties, the more necessary to try to remove them." As sentiment strengthens, it undermines obstacles, and they crumble before it.

The same tendency is shown in the undeniable disposition of the British people and of British statesmen to cultivate the good-will of the United States, and to draw closer the relations between the two countries. For the disposition underlying such a tendency Mr. Balfour has used an expression, " race patriotism," — a phrase which finds its first approximation, doubtless, in the English-speaking family, but which may well extend its embrace, in a time

17

yet distant, to all those who have drawn their
present civilization from the same remote
sources. The phrase is so pregnant of solution
for the problems of the future, as conceived by
the writer, that he hopes to see it obtain the
currency due to the value of the idea which it
formulates. That this disposition on the part
of Great Britain, towards her colonies and
towards the United States, shows sound policy
as well as sentiment, may be granted readily;
but why should sound policy, the seeking of
one's own advantage, if by open and honest
means, be imputed as a crime? In democracies, however, policy cannot long dispute the
sceptre with sentiment. That there is luke-
warm response in the United States is due to
that narrow conception which grew up with
the middle of the century, whose analogue in
Great Britain is the Little England party, and
which in our own country would turn all eyes
inward, and see no duty save to ourselves.
How shall two walk together except they be
agreed? How shall there be true sympathy
between a nation whose political activities are
world-wide, and one that eats out its heart in
merely internal political strife? When we

begin really to look abroad, and to busy ourselves with our duties to the world at large in
our generation — and not before — we shall
stretch out our hands to Great Britain, realizing that in unity of heart among the English-
speaking races lies the best hope of humanity
in the doubtful days ahead.

In the determination of the duties of nations,
nearness is the most conspicuous and the most
general indication. Considering the American
states as members of the European family, as
they are by traditions, institutions, and lan-
guages, it is in the Pacific, where the westward
course of empire again meets the East, that
their relations to the future of the world
become most apparent. The Atlantic, bordered on either shore by the European family
in the strongest and most advanced types of its
political development, no longer severs, but
binds together, by all the facilities and abundance of water communications, the once
divided children of the same mother; the in-
heritors of Greece and Rome, and of the Teutonic conquerors of the latter. A limited
express or a flying freight may carry a few pas-
sengers or a small bulk overland from the

Atlantic to the Pacific more rapidly than modern steamers can cross the former ocean, but for the vast amounts in numbers or in quantity which are required for the full fruition of communication, it is the land that divides, and not the sea. On the Pacific coast, severed from their brethren by desert and mountain range, are found the outposts, the exposed pioneers of European civilization, whom it is one of the first duties of the European family to bind more closely to the main body, and to protect, by due foresight over the approaches to them on either side.

It is in this political fact, and not in the weighing of merely commercial advantages, that is to be found the great significance of the future canal across the Central American isthmus, as well as the importance of the Caribbean Sea; for the latter is inseparably intwined with all international consideration of the isthmus problem. Wherever situated, whether at Panama or at Nicaragua, the fundamental meaning of the canal will be that it advances by thousands of miles the frontiers of European civilization in general, and of the United States in particular; that it knits together the whole system of American states enjoying that civilization as in no other way they can be bound. In the Caribbean Archipelago — the very domain of sea power, if ever region could be called so — are the natural home and centre of those influences by which such a maritime highway as a canal must be controlled, even as the control of the Suez Canal rests in the Mediterranean. Hawaii, too, is an outpost of the canal, as surely as Aden or Malta is of Suez; or as Malta was of India in the days long before the canal, when Nelson proclaimed that in that point of view chiefly was it important to Great Britain. In the cluster of island fortresses of the Caribbean is one of the greatest of the nerve centres of the whole body of European civilization; and it is to be regretted that so serious a portion of them now is in hands which not only never have given, but to all appearances never can give, the development which is required by the general interest.

For what awaits us in the future, in common with the states of Europe, is not a mere question of advantage or disadvantage — of more or less. Issues of vital moment are involved. A present generation is trustee for its succes-

sors, and may be faithless to its charge quite
as truly by inaction as by action, by omission
as by commission. Failure to improve opportunity, where just occasion arises, may entail
upon posterity problems and difficulties which,
if overcome at all — it may then be too late —
will be so at the cost of blood and tears that
timely foresight might have spared. Such
preventive measures, if taken, are in no true
sense offensive but defensive. Decadent conditions, such as we observe in Turkey — and
not in Turkey alone — cannot be indefinitely
prolonged by opportunist counsels or timid
procrastination. A time comes in human
affairs, as in physical ailments, when heroic
measures must be used to save the life of a
patient or the welfare of a community; and if
that time is allowed to pass, as many now
think that it was at the time of the Crimean
war, the last state is worse than the first, — an
opinion which these passing days of the hesitancy of the Concert and the anguish of
Greece, not to speak of the Armenian outrages,
surely indorse. Europe, advancing in distant
regions, still allows to exist in her own side,
unexcised, a sore that may yet drain her life-

blood ; still leaves in recognized dominion, over fair regions of great future import, a system whose hopelessness of political and social improvement the lapse of time renders continually more certain, — an evil augury for the future, if a turning tide shall find it unchanged, an outpost of barbarism ready for alien occupation.

It is essential to our own good, it is yet more essential as part of our duty to the commonwealth of peoples to which we racially belong, that we look with clear, dispassionate, but resolute eyes upon the fact that civilizations on different planes of material prosperity and progress, with different spiritual ideals, and with very different political capacities, are fast closing together. It is a condition not unprecedented in the history of the world. When it befell a great united empire, enervated by long years of unwarlike habits among its chief citizens, it entailed ruin, but ruin deferred through centuries, thanks to the provision made beforehand by a great general and statesman. The Saracenic and Turkish invasions, on the contrary, after generations of advance, were first checked, and then rolled back; for they fell upon peoples, disunited indeed by internal discords and strife, like the nations of Europe to-day, but still nations of warriors, ready by training and habit to strike for their rights, and, if need were, to die for them. In the providence of God, along with the immense increase of prosperity, of physical and mental luxury, brought by this century, there has grown up also that counterpoise stigmatized as "militarism," which has converted Europe into a great camp of soldiers prepared for war. The ill-timed cry for disarmament, heedless of the menacing possibilities of the future, breaks idly against a great fact, which finds its sufficient justification in present conditions, but which is, above all, an unconscious preparation for something as yet noted but by few.

On the side of the land, these great armies, and the blind outward impulse of the European peoples, are the assurance that generations must elapse ere the barriers can be overcome behind which rests the citadel of Christian civilization. On the side of the sea there is no state charged with weightier responsibilities than the United States. In the Caribbean, the sensitive resentment by our people of any supposed fresh encroachment by another state of the European family has been manifested too plainly and too recently to admit of dispute. Such an attitude of itself demands of us to be ready to support it by organized force, exactly as the mutual jealousy of states within the European Continent imposes upon them the maintenance of their great armies — destined, we believe, in the future, to fulfil a nobler mission. Where we thus exclude others, we accept for ourselves the responsibility for that which is due to the general family of our civilization; and the Caribbean Sea, with its isthmus, is the nexus where will meet the chords binding the East to the West, the Atlantic to the Pacific.

The Isthmus, with all that depends upon it, — its canal and its approaches on either hand, — will link the eastern side of the American continent to the western as no network of land communications ever can. In it the United States has asserted a special interest. In the present she can maintain her claim, and in the future perform her duty, only by the creation of that sea power upon which predominance in the Caribbean must ever depend. In short, as the internal jealousies of Europe, and the purely democratic institution of the *levée en masse* — the general enforcement of military training — have prepared the way for great national armies, whose mission seems yet obscure, so the gradual broadening and tightening hold upon the sentiment of American democracy of that conviction loosely characterized as the Monroe doctrine finds its logical and inevitable outcome in a great sea power, the correlative, in connection with that of Great Britain, of those armies which continue to flourish under the most popular institutions, despite the wails of economists and the lamentations of those who wish peace without paying the one price which alone has ever insured peace, — readiness for war.

Thus it was, while readiness for war lasted, that the Teuton was held back until he became civilized, humanized, after the standard of that age; till the root of the matter was in him, sure to bear fruit in due season. He was held back by organized armed force — by armies. Will it be said that that was in a past barbaric age? Barbarism, however, is not in more or less material prosperity, or even political development, but in the inner man, in the spiritual ideal; and the material, which comes first and has in itself no salt of life to save from corruption, must be controlled by other material forces, until the spiritual can find room and time to germinate. We need not fear but that that which appeals to the senses in our civilization will be appropriated, even though it be necessary to destroy us, if disarmed, in order to obtain it. Our own civilization less its spiritual element is barbarism; and barbarism will be the civilization of those who assimilate its material progress without imbibing the indwelling spirit.

Let us worship peace, indeed, as the goal at which humanity must hope to arrive; but let us not fancy that peace is to be had as a boy wrenches an unripe fruit from a tree. Nor will peace be reached by ignoring the conditions that confront us, or by exaggerating the charms of quiet, of prosperity, of ease, and by contrasting these exclusively with the alarms and horrors of war. Merely utilitarian arguments have never convinced nor converted mankind, and they never will; for mankind knows that there is something better. Its homage will never be commanded by peace, presented as the tutelary deity of the stock-market.

Nothing is more ominous for the future of our race than that tendency, vociferous at present, which refuses to recognize in the profession of arms, in war, that something which inspired Wordsworth's "Happy Warrior," which soothed the dying hours of Henry Lawrence, who framed the ideals of his career on the poet's conception, and so nobly illustrated it in his self-sacrifice; that something which has made the soldier to all ages the type of heroism and of self-denial. When the religion of Christ, of Him who was led as a lamb to the slaughter, seeks to raise before its followers the image of self-control, and of resistance to evil, it is the soldier whom it presents. He Himself, if by office King of Peace, is, first of all, in the essence of His Being, King of Righteousness, without which true peace cannot be.

Conflict is the condition of all life, material and spiritual; and it is to the soldier's experience that the spiritual life goes for its most vivid metaphors and its loftiest inspirations. Whatever else the twentieth century may bring us, it will not, from anything now current in the thought of the nineteenth, receive a nobler ideal.

THE STRATEGIC FEATURES OF THE GULF OF MEXICO AND THE CARIBBEAN SEA.

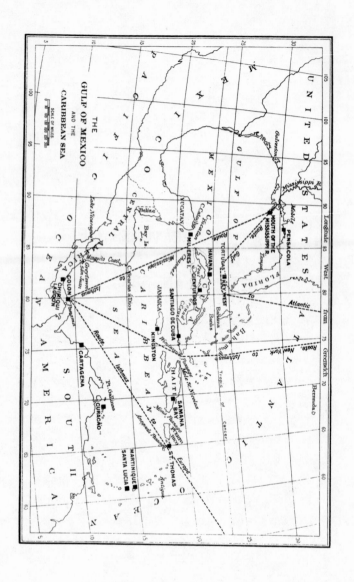

THE
GULF OF MEXICO
AND THE
CARIBBEAN SEA

SCALE OF MILES

THE STRATEGIC FEATURES OF THE GULF OF MEXICO AND THE CARIBBEAN SEA.

June, 1897.

THE importance, absolute and relative, of portions of the earth's surface, and their consequent interest to mankind, vary from time to time. The Mediterranean was for many ages the centre round which gathered all the influences and developments of those earlier civilizations from which our own, mediately or immediately, derives. During the chaotic period of struggle that intervened between their fall and the dawn of our modern conditions, the Inland Sea, through its hold upon the traditions and culture of antiquity, still retained a general ascendency, although at length its political predominance was challenged, and finally overcome, by the younger, more virile, and more warlike nationalities that had been forming gradually beyond the Alps, and on the shores of the Atlantic and Northern oceans. It was, until the close of the Middle Ages, the one route by which the East and the West maintained commercial relations; for, although the trade eastward from the Levant was by long and painful land journeys, over mountain range and desert plain, water communication, in part and up to that point, was afforded by the Mediterranean, and by it alone. With the discovery of the passage by the Cape of Good Hope this advantage departed, while at the same instant the discovery of a New World opened out to the Old new elements of luxury and a new sphere of ambition. Then the Mediterranean, thrown upon its own productive resources alone, swayed in the East by the hopeless barbarism of the Turk, in the West by the decadent despotism of Spain, and, between the two, divided among a number of petty states, incapable of united and consequently of potent action, sank into a factor of relatively small consequence to the onward progress of the world. During the wars of the French Revolution, when the life of Great Britain, and consequently the issue of the strife, depended upon the vigor of British commerce, British merchant shipping was nearly driven from that sea; and but two per cent of a trade that was increasing mightily all the time was thence derived. How the Suez Canal and the growth of the Eastern Question, in its modern form, have changed all that, it is needless to say. Yet, through all the period of relative insignificance, the relations of the Mediterranean to the East and to the West, in the broad sense of those expressions, pre-served to it a political importance to the world at large which rendered it continuously a scene of great political ambitions and military enter-prise. Since Great Britain first actively inter-vened in those waters, two centuries ago, she at no time has surrendered willingly her pre-tensions to be a leading Mediterranean Power, although her possessions there are of purely military, or rather naval, value.

The Caribbean Sea and the Gulf of Mexico, taken together, form an inland sea and an archipelago. They too have known those mu-tabilities of fortune which receive illustration alike in the history of countries and in the lives of individuals. The first scene of dis-covery and of conquest in the New World, these twin sheets of water, with their islands

18

and their mainlands, became for many generations, and nearly to our own time, a veritable El Dorado, — a land where the least of labor, on the part of its new possessors, rendered the largest and richest returns. The bounty of nature, and the ease with which climatic conditions, aided by the unwarlike character of most of the natives, adapted themselves to the institution of slavery, insured the cheap and abundant production of articles which, when once enjoyed, men found indispensable, as they already had the silks and spices of the East. In Mexico and in Peru were realized also, in degree, the actual gold-mine sought by the avarice of the earlier Spanish explorers; while a short though difficult tropical journey brought the treasures of the west coast across the Isthmus to the shores of the broad ocean, nature's great highway, which washed at once the shores of Old and of New Spain.   From the Caribbean, Great Britain, although her rivals had anticipated her in the possession of the largest and richest districts, derived nearly twenty-five per cent of her commerce, during the strenuous period when the Mediterranean contributed but two per cent.

But over these fair regions too passed the blight, not of despotism merely, for despotism was characteristic of the times, but of a despotism which found no counteractive, no element of future deliverance, in the temperament or in the political capacities of the people over whom it ruled. Elizabeth, as far as she dared, was a despot; Philip II. was a despot; but there was already manifest in her subjects, while there was not in his, a will and a power not merely to resist oppression, but to organize freedom. This will and this power, after gaining many partial victories by the way, culminated once for all in the American Revolution. Great Britain has never forgotten the lesson then taught; for it was one she herself had been teaching for centuries, and her people and statesmen were therefore easy learners. A century and a quarter has passed since that warning was given, not to Great Britain only, but to the world; and we to-day see, in the contrasted colonial systems of the two states, the results, on the one hand of political aptitude, on the other of political obtuseness and backwardness, which cannot struggle from the past into the present until the present in turn has become the past — irreclaimable.

Causes superficially very diverse but essentially the same, in that they arose from and still depend upon a lack of local political capacity, have brought the Mediterranean and the Caribbean, in our own time, to similar conditions, regarded as quantities of interest in the sphere of international relations. Whatever the intrinsic value of the two bodies of water, in themselves or in their surroundings, whatever their present contributions to the prosperity or to the culture of mankind, their conspicuous characteristics now are their political and military importance, in the broadest sense, as concerning not only the countries that border them, but the world at large. Both are land-girt seas; both are links in a chain of communication between an East and a West; in both the chain is broken by an isthmus; both are of contracted extent when compared with great oceans, and, in consequence of these common features, both present in an intensified form the advantages and the limitations, political and military, which condition the influence of sea power. This conclusion is notably true of the Mediterranean, as is shown by its history. It is even more forcibly true of the Caribbean, partly because the contour of its shores does not, as in the Mediterranean peninsulas, thrust the power of the land so far and so sustainedly into the sea; partly because, from historical antecedents already alluded to, in the character of the first colonists, and from the shortness of the time the ground has been in civilized occupation, there does not exist in the Caribbean or in the Gulf of Mexico — apart from the United States — any land power at all comparable with those great Continental states of Europe whose strength lies in their armies far more than in their navies. So far as national inclinations, as distinct from the cautious actions of statesmen, can be discerned, in the Mediterranean at present the Sea Powers, Great Britain, France, and Italy, are opposed to the Land Powers, Germany, Austria, and Russia; and the latter dominate action. It cannot be so, in any near future, in the Caribbean. As affirmed in a previous paper, the Caribbean is pre-eminently the domain of sea power. It is in this point of view — the military or naval — that it is now to be considered. Its political importance will be assumed, as recognized by our forefathers, and enforced upon our own attention by the sudden apprehensions awakened within the last two years.

It may be well, though possibly needless, to ask readers to keep clearly in mind that the Caribbean Sea and the Gulf of Mexico, while knit together like the Siamese twins, are distinct geographical entities. A leading British periodical once accused the writer of calling the Gulf of Mexico the Caribbean Sea, because of his unwillingness to admit the name of any other state in connection with a body of water over which his own country claimed predominance. The Gulf of Mexico is very clearly defined by the projection, from the north, of the peninsula of Florida, and from the south, of that of Yucatan. Between the two the island of Cuba interposes for a distance of two hundred miles, leaving on one side a passage of nearly a hundred miles wide — the Strait of Florida — into the Atlantic, while on the other, the Yucatan Channel, somewhat broader, leads into the Caribbean Sea. It may be mentioned here, as an important military consideration, that from the mouth of the Mississippi westward to Cape Catoche — the tip of the Yucatan Peninsula — there is no harbor that can be considered at all satisfactory for ships of war of the larger classes. The existence of many such harbors in other parts of the regions now under consideration practically eliminates this long stretch of coast, regarded as a factor of military importance in the problem before us.

In each of these sheets of water, the Gulf of Mexico and the Caribbean, there is one position of pre-eminent commercial importance. In the Gulf the mouth of the Mississippi is the point where meet all the exports and imports, by water, of the Mississippi Valley. However diverse the directions from which they come, or the destinations to which they proceed, all come together here as at a great crossroads, or as the highways of an empire converge on the metropolis. Whatever value the Mississippi and the myriad miles of its subsidiary water-courses represent to the United States, as a facile means of communication from the remote interior to the ocean highways of the world, all centres here at the mouth of the river. The existence of the smaller though important cities of the Gulf coast— Mobile, Galveston, or the Mexican ports — does not diminish, but rather emphasizes by contrast, the importance of the Mississippi entrance. They all share its fortunes, in that all alike communicate with the outside world through the Strait of Florida or the Yucatan Channel.

In the Caribbean, likewise, the existence of numerous important ports, and a busy traffic in tropical produce grown within the region itself, do but make more striking the predominance in interest of that one position known comprehensively, but up to the present somewhat indeterminately, as the Isthmus. Here again the element of decisive value is the crossing of the roads, the meeting of the ways, which, whether imposed by nature itself, as in the cases before us, or induced, as sometimes happens, in a less degree, by simple human dispositions, are prime factors in mercantile or strategic consequence. For these reasons the Isthmus, even under the disadvantages of land carriage and transshipment of goods, has ever been an important link in the communications from East to West, from the days of the first discoverers and throughout all subsequent centuries, though fluctuating in degree from age to age; but when it shall be pierced by a canal, it will present a maritime centre analogous to the mouth of the Mississippi. They will differ in this, that in the latter case the converging water routes on one side are interior to a great state whose resources they bear, whereas the roads which on either side converge upon the Isthmus lie wholly upon the ocean, the common possession of all nations. Control of the latter, therefore, rests either upon local control of the Isthmus itself, or, indirectly, upon control of its approaches, or upon a distinctly preponderant navy. In naval questions the latter is always the dominant factor, exactly as on land the mobile army — the army in the field — must dominate the question of fortresses, unless war is to be impotent.

We have thus the two centres round which revolve all the military study of the Caribbean Sea and the Gulf of Mexico. The two sheets of water, taken together, control or affect the approaches on one side to these two supreme centres of commercial, and therefore of political and military, interest. The approaches on the other side — the interior communications of the Mississippi, that is, or the maritime routes in the Pacific converging upon the Isthmus — do not here concern us. These approaches, in terms of military art, are known as the "communications." Communications are probably the most vital and determining element in strategy, military or naval. They are literally the most radical; for all military operations depend upon communications, as the fruit of a plant depends upon communication with its root. We draw therefore upon the map the chief lines by which communication exists between these two centres and the outside world. Such lines represent the mutual dependence of the centres and the exterior, by which each ministers to the others, and by severance of which either becomes useless to the others. It is from their potential effect upon these lines of communication that all positions in the Gulf or the Caribbean derive their military value, or want of value.

It is impossible to precede or to accompany a discussion of this sort with a technical exposition of naval strategy. Such definitions of the art as may be needed must be given *in loco*, cursorily and dogmatically. Therefore it will be said here briefly that the strategic value of any position, be it body of land large or small, or a seaport, or a strait, depends, 1, upon situation (with reference chiefly to communications), 2, upon its strength (inherent or acquired), and, 3, upon its resources (natural or stored). As strength and resources are matters which man can accumulate where suitable situation offers, whereas he cannot change the location of a place in itself otherwise advantageous, it is upon situation that attention must primarily be fixed. Strength and resources may be artificially supplied or increased, but it passes the power of man to move a port which lies outside the limits of strategic effect. Gibraltar in mid-ocean might have fourfold its present power, yet would be valueless in a military sense.

The positions which are indicated on the map by the dark squares have been selected, therefore, upon these considerations, after a careful study of the inherent advantages of the various ports and coast-lines of the Caribbean Sea and the Gulf. It is by no means meant that there are not others which possess merits of various kinds; or that those indicated, and to be named, exhaust the strategic possibilities of the region under examination. But there are qualifying circumstances of degree in particular cases; and a certain regard must be had to political conditions, which may be said to a great extent to neutralize some positions. Some, too, are excluded because overshadowed by others so near and so strong as practically to embrace them, when under the same political tenure. Moreover, it is a commonplace of strategy that passive positions, fortified places, however strong, although indispensable as supports to military operations, should not be held in great number. To do so wastes force. Similarly, in the study of a field of maritime operations, the number of available positions, whose relative and combined influence upon the whole is to be considered, should be narrowed, by a process of gradual elimination, to those clearly essential and representative. To embrace more confuses the attention, wastes mental force, and is a hindrance to correct appreciation. The rejection of details, where permissible, and understandingly done, facilitates comprehension, which is baffled by a multiplication of minutiæ, just as the impression of a work of art, or of a story, is lost amid a multiplicity of figures or of actors. The investigation precedent to formulation of ideas must be close and minute, but that done, the unbiassed selection of the most important, expressed graphically by a few lines and a few dots, leads most certainly to the comprehension of decisive relations in a military field of action.

In the United States, Pensacola and the Mississippi River have been rivals for the possession of a navy-yard. The recent decision of a specially appointed board in favor of the latter, while it commands the full assent of the writer, by no means eliminates the usefulness of the former. Taken together, they fulfil a fair requirement of strategy, sea and land, that operations based upon a national frontier, which a coast-line is, should not depend upon a single place only. They are closer together than ideal perfection would wish; too easily, therefore, to be watched by an enemy without great dispersal of his force, which Norfolk and New York, for instance, are not; but still, conjointly, they are the best we can do on that line, having regard to the draught of water for heavy ships. Key West, an island lying off the end of the Florida Peninsula, has long been recognized as the chief, and almost the only, good and defensible anchorage upon the Strait of Florida, reasonable control of which is indispensable to water communication between our Atlantic and Gulf seaboards in time of war. In case of war in the direction of the Caribbean, Key West is the extreme point now in our possession upon which, granting adequate fortification, our fleets could rely; and, so used, it would effectually divert an enemy's force from Pensacola and the Mississippi. It can never be the ultimate base of operations, as Pensacola or New Orleans can, because it is an island, a small island, and has no resources — not even water; but for the daily needs of a fleet — coal, ammunition, etc. — it can be made most effective. Sixty miles west of it stands an antiquated fortress on the Dry Tortugas. These are capable of being made a useful adjunct to Key West, but at present they scarcely can be so considered. Key West is 550 miles distant from the mouth of the Mississippi, and 1200 from the Isthmus.

The islands of Santa Lucia and of Martinique have been selected because they represent the chief positions of, respectively, Great Britain and France on the outer limits of the general field under consideration. For the reasons already stated, Grenada, Barbadoes, Dominica, and the other near British islands are not taken into account, or rather are considered to be embraced in Santa Lucia, which adequately represents them. If a secondary position on that line were required, it would be at Antigua, which would play to Santa Lucia the part which Pensacola does to the Mississippi. In like manner the French Guadeloupe merges in Martinique. The intrinsic importance of these positions consists in the fact that, being otherwise suitable and properly defended, they are the nearest to the mother-countries, between whom and themselves there lies no point of danger near which it is necessary to pass. They have the disadvantage of being very small islands, consequently without adequate natural resources, and easy to be blockaded on all sides. They are therefore essentially dependent for their usefulness in war upon control of the sea, which neither

Pensacola nor New Orleans is, having the continent at their backs.

It is in this respect that the pre-eminent intrinsic advantages of Cuba, or rather of Spain in Cuba, are to be seen; and also, but in much less degree, those of Great Britain in Jamaica. Cuba, though narrow throughout, is over six hundred miles long, from Cape San Antonio to Cape Maysi. It is, in short, not so much an island as a continent, susceptible, under proper development, of great resources — of self-sufficingness. In area it is half as large again as Ireland, but, owing to its peculiar form, is much more than twice as long. Marine distances, therefore, are drawn out to an extreme degree. Its many natural harbors concentrate themselves, to a military examination, into three principal groups, whose representatives are, in the west, Havana; in the east, Santiago; while near midway of the southern shore lies Cienfuegos. The shortest water distance separating any two of these is 335 miles, from Santiago to Cienfuegos. To get from Cienfuegos to Havana 450 miles of water must be traversed and the western point of the island doubled; yet the two ports are distant by land only a little more than a hundred miles of fairly easy country. Regarded, therefore, as a base of naval operations, as a source of supplies to a fleet, Cuba presents a condition wholly unique among the islands of the Caribbean and of the Gulf of Mexico; to both which it, and it alone of all the archipelago, belongs. It is unique in its size, which should render it largely self-supporting, either by its own products, or by the accumulation of foreign necessaries which naturally obtains in a large and prosperous maritime community; and it is unique in that such supplies can be conveyed from one point to the other, according to the needs of a fleet, by interior lines, not exposed to risks of maritime capture. The extent of the coast-line, the numerous harbors, and the many directions from which approach can be made, minimize the dangers of total blockade, to which all islands are subject. Such conditions are in themselves advantageous, but they are especially so to a navy inferior to its adversary, for they convey the power — subject, of course, to conditions of skill — of shifting operations from side to side, and finding refuge and supplies in either direction.

Jamaica, being but one-tenth the size of Cuba, and one-fifth of its length, does not present the intrinsic advantages of the latter island, regarded either as a source of supplies or as a centre from which to direct effort; but when in the hands of a power supreme at sea, as at the present Great Britain is, the questions of supplies, of blockade, and of facility in direction of effort diminish in importance. That which in the one case is a matter of life and death, becomes now only an embarrassing problem, necessitating watchfulness and precaution, but by no means insoluble. No advantages of position can counterbalance, in the long-run, decisive inferiority in organized mobile force, — inferiority in troops in the field, and yet much more in ships on the sea. If Spain should become involved in war with Great Britain, as she so often before has been, the advantage she would have in Cuba as against Jamaica would be that her communications with the United States, especially with the Gulf ports, would be well under cover. By this is not meant that vessels bound to Cuba by such routes would be in unassailable security; no communications, maritime or terrestrial, can be so against raiding. What is meant is that they can be protected with much less effort than they can be attacked; that the raiders — the offence — must be much more numerous and active than the defence, because much farther from their base; and that the question of such raiding would depend consequently upon the force Great Britain could spare from other scenes of war, for it is not likely that Spain would fight her single-handed. It is quite possible that under such conditions advantage of position would more than counterbalance a *small* disadvantage in local force. "War," said Napoleon, "is a business of positions;" by which that master of lightning-like rapidity of movement assuredly did not mean that it was a business of getting into a position and sticking there. It is in the utilization of position by mobile force that war is determined, just as the effect of a chessman depends upon both its individual value *and* its relative position. While, therefore, in the combination of the two factors, force and position, force is intrinsically the more valuable, it is always possible that great advantage of position may outweigh small advantage of force, as $1 + 5$ is greater than $2 + 3$. The positional value of Cuba is extremely great.

Regarded solely as a naval position, without reference to the force thereon based, Jamaica is greatly inferior to Cuba in a question of general war, notwithstanding the fact that in Kingston it possesses an excellent harbor and naval station. It is only with direct reference to the Isthmus, and therefore to the local question of the Caribbean as the main scene of hostilities, that it possesses a certain superiority which will be touched on later. It is advisable first to complete the list, and so far as necessary to account for the selection, of the other points indicated by the squares.

Of these, three are so nearly together at the Isthmus that, according to the rule before adopted, they might be reduced very properly to a single representative position. Being, however, so close to the great centre of interest in the Caribbean, and having different specific reasons constituting their importance, it is essential to a full statement of strategic conditions in that sea to mention briefly each and all. They are, the harbor and town of Colon, sometimes called Aspinwall; the harbor and city of Cartagena, 300 miles to the eastward of Colon; and the Chiriqui Lagoon, 150 miles west of Colon, a vast enclosed bay with many islands, giving excellent and diversified anchorage, the shores of which are nearly uninhabited. Colon is the Caribbean terminus of the Panama Railroad, and is also that of the canal projected, and partly dug, under the De Lesseps scheme. The harbor being good, though open to some winds, it is naturally indicated as a point where Isthmian transit may begin or end. As there is no intention of entering into the controversy about the relative merits of the Panama and Nicaragua canal schemes, it will be sufficient here to say that, if the former be carried through, Colon is its inevitable issue on one side. The city of Cartagena is the largest and most flourishing in the neighborhood of the Isthmus, and has a good harbor. With these conditions obtaining, its advantage rests upon the axiomatic principle that, other things being nearly equal, a place where commerce centres is a better strategic position than one which it neglects. The latter is the condition of the Chiriqui Lagoon. This truly noble sheet of water, which was visited by

Columbus himself, and bears record of the fact in the name of one of its basins, — the Bay of the Admiral, — has every natural adaptation for a purely naval base, but has not drawn to itself the operations of commerce. Everything would need there to be created, and to be maintained continuously. It lies midway between Colon and the mouth of the river San Juan, where is Greytown, which has been selected as the issue of the projected Nicaragua Canal; and therefore, in a peculiar way, Chiriqui symbolizes the present indeterminate phase of the Isthmian problem. With all its latent possibilities, however, little can be said now of Chiriqui, except that a rough appreciation of its existence and character is essential to an adequate understanding of Isthmian conditions.

The Dutch island of Curaçao has been marked, chiefly because, with its natural characteristics, it cannot be passed over; but it now is, and it may be hoped will remain indefinitely, among the positions of which it has been said that they are neutralized by political circumstances. Curaçao possesses a fine harbor, which may be made impregnable, and it lies unavoidably near the route of any vessel bound to the Isthmus and passing eastward of Jamaica. Such conditions constitute undeniable military importance; but Holland is a small state, unlikely to join again in a general war. There is, indeed, a floating apprehension that the German Empire, in its present desires of colonial extension, may be willing to absorb Holland, for the sake of her still extensive colonial possessions. Improbable as this may seem, it is scarcely more incomprehensible than the recent mysterious movements upon the European chess-board, attributed by common rumor to the dominating influence of the Emperor of Germany, which we puzzled Americans for months past have sought in vain to understand.

The same probable neutrality must be admitted for the remaining positions that have been distinguished: Mujeres Island, Samana Bay, and the island of St. Thomas. The first of these, at the extremity of the Yucatan Peninsula, belongs to Mexico, a country whose interest in the Isthmian question is very real; for, like the United States, she has an extensive seaboard both upon the Pacific and — in the Gulf of Mexico — upon the Atlantic Ocean.

Mujeres Island, however, has nothing to offer but situation, being upon the Yucatan Passage, the one road from all the Gulf ports to the Caribbean and the Isthmus. The anchorage is barely tolerable, the resources *nil*, and defensive strength could be imparted only by an expense quite disproportionate to the result obtained. The consideration of the island as a possible military situation does but emphasize the fact, salient to the most superficial glance, that, so far as position goes, Cuba has no possible rival in her command of the Yucatan Passage, just as she has no competitor, in point of natural strength and resources, for the control of the Florida Strait, which connects the Gulf of Mexico with the Atlantic.

Samana Bay, at the northeast corner of Santo Domingo, is but one of several fine anchorages in that great island, whose territory is now divided between two negro republics — French and Spanish in tongue. Its selection to figure in our study, to the exclusion of the others, is determined by its situation, and by the fact that we are seeking to take a comprehensive glance of the Caribbean as a whole, and not merely of particular districts. For instance, it might be urged forcibly, in view of the existence of two great naval ports like Santiago de Cuba and Port Royal in Jamaica, close to the Windward Passage, through which lies the direct route from the Atlantic seaboard to the Isthmus, that St. Nicholas Mole, immediately on the Passage, offers the natural position for checking the others in case of need. The reply is that we are not seeking to check anything or anybody, but simply examining in the large the natural strategic features, and incidentally thereto noting the political conditions, of a maritime region in which the United States is particularly interested ; political conditions, as has been remarked, having an unavoidable effect upon military values.

The inquiry being thus broad, Samana Bay and the island of St. Thomas are entitled to the pre-eminence here given to them, because they represent, efficiently and better than any other positions, the control of two principal passages into the Caribbean Sea from the Atlantic. The Mona Passage, on which Samana lies, between Santo Domingo and Puerto Rico, is particularly suited to sailing-vessels from the northward, because free from dangers to navigation. This, of course, in these days of steam, is a small matter militarily; in the latter sense the Mona Passage is valuable because it is an alternative to the Windward Passage, or to those to the eastward, in case of hostile predominance in one quarter or the other. St. Thomas is on the Anegada Passage, actually much used, and which better than any other represents the course from Europe to the Isthmus, just as the Windward Passage does that from the North American Atlantic ports. Neither of these places can boast of great natural strength nor of resources; St. Thomas, because it is a small island with the inherent weaknesses attending all such, which have been mentioned; Samana Bay, because, although the island on which it is is large and productive, it has not now, and gives no hope of having, that political stability and commercial prosperity which bring resources and power in their train. Both places would need also considerable development of defensive works to meet the requirements of a naval port. Despite these defects, their situations on the passages named entitle them to paramount consideration in a general study of the Caribbean

Sea and the Gulf of Mexico. Potentially, though not actually, they lend control of the Mona and Anegada Passages, exactly as Kingston and Santiago do of the Windward.

For, granting that the Isthmus is in the Caribbean the predominant interest, commercial, and therefore concerning the whole world, but also military, and so far possessing peculiar concern for those nations whose territories lie on both oceans, which it now severs and will one day unite — of which nations the United States is the most prominent — granting this, and it follows that entrance to the Caribbean, and transit across the Caribbean to the Isthmus, are two prime essentials to the enjoyment of the advantages of the latter. Therefore, in case of war, control of these two things becomes a military object not second to the Isthmus itself, access to which depends upon them; and in their bearing upon these two things the various positions that are passed under consideration must be viewed — individually first, and afterwards collectively.

The first process of individual consideration the writer has asked the reader to take on faith; neither time nor space permits its elaboration here; but the reasons for choosing those that have been named have been given as briefly as possible. Let us now look at the map, and regard as a collective whole the picture there graphically presented.

Putting to one side, for the moment at least, the Isthmian points, as indicating the end rather than the precedent means, we see at the present time that the positions at the extremes of the field under examination are held by Powers of the first rank, — Martinique and Santa Lucia by France and Great Britain, Pensacola and the Mississippi by the United States.

Further, there are held by these same states of the first order two advanced positions, widely separated from the first bases of their power; namely, Key West, which is 460 miles from Pensacola, and Jamaica, which is 930 miles from Santa Lucia. From the Isthmus, Key West is distant 1200 miles; Jamaica, 500 miles.

Between and separating these two groups, of primary bases and advanced posts, extends the chain of positions from Yucatan to St. Thomas. As far as is possible to position, apart from mobile force, these represent control over the northern entrances — the most important entrances — into the Caribbean Sea. No one of this chain belongs to any of the Powers commonly reckoned as being of the first order of strength.

The entrances on the north of the sea, as far as, but not including, the Anegada Passage, are called the most important, because they are so few in number, — a circumstance which always increases value; because they are so much nearer to the Isthmus; and, very especially to the United States, because they are the ones by which, and by which alone, — except at the cost of a wide ·circuit, — she communicates with the Isthmus, and, generally, with all the region lying within the borders of the Caribbean.

In a very literal sense the Caribbean is a mediterranean sea; but the adjective must be qualified when comparison is made with the Mediterranean of the Old World or with the Gulf of Mexico. The last-named bodies of water communicate with the outer oceans by passages so contracted as to be easily watched from near-by positions, and for both there exist such positions of exceptional strength, — Gibraltar and some others in the former case, Havana and no other in the latter. The Caribbean, on the contrary, is enclosed on its eastern side by a chain of small islands, the passages between which, although practically not wider than the Strait of Gibraltar, are so numerous that entrance to the sea on that side may be said correctly to extend over a stretch of near 400 miles. The islands, it is true, are so many positions, some better, some worse, from which military effort to control entrance can be exerted; but their number prevents that concentration and that certainty of effect which are possible to adequate force resting upon Gibraltar or Havana.

On the northern side of the sea the case is quite different. From the western end of Cuba to the eastern end of Puerto Rico extends a barrier of land for 1200 miles — as against 400 on the east — broken only by two straits, each fifty miles wide, from side to side of which a steamer of but moderate power can pass in three or four hours. These natural conditions, governing the approach to the Isthmus, reproduce as nearly as possible the strategic effect of Ireland upon Great Britain. There a land barrier of 300 miles, midway between the Pentland Firth and the English Channel — centrally situated, that is, with reference to all the Atlantic approaches to Great Britain — gives to an adequate navy a unique power to flank and harass either the one or the other, or both. Existing political conditions and other circumstances unquestionably modify the importance of these two barriers, relatively to the countries affected by them. Open communication with the Atlantic is vital to Great Britain, which the Isthmus, up to the present time, is not to the United States. There are, however, varying degrees of importance below that which is vital. Taking into consideration that of the 1200-mile barrier to the Caribbean 600 miles is solid in Cuba, that after the 50-mile gap of the Windward Passage there succeeds 300 miles more of Haiti before the Mona Passage is reached, it is indisputable that a superior navy, resting on Santiago de Cuba or Jamaica, could very seriously incommode all access of the United States to the Caribbean mainland, and especially to the Isthmus.

In connection with this should be considered also the influence upon our mercantile and naval communication between the Atlantic and the Gulf coasts exercised by the peninsula of Florida, and by the narrowness of the channels separating the latter from the Bahama Banks and from Cuba. The effect of this long and not very broad strip of land upon our maritime interests can be realized best by imagining it wholly removed, or else turned into an island by a practicable channel crossing its neck. In the latter case the two entrances to the channel would have indeed to be assured; but our shipping would not be forced to pass through a long, narrow waterway, bordered throughout on one side by foreign and possibly hostile territories. In case of war with either Great Britain or Spain, this channel would be likely to be infested by hostile cruisers, close to their own base, the very best condition for a commerce-destroying war; and its protection by us under present circumstances will exact a much greater effort than with the supposed channel, or than if the Florida Peninsula did not exist. The effect of the peninsula is to thrust our route from the Atlantic to the Gulf

300 miles to the southward, and to make imperative a base for control of the strait; while the case is made worse by an almost total lack of useful harbors. On the Atlantic, the most exposed side, there is none; and on the Gulf none nearer to Key West than 175 miles,[1] where we find Tampa Bay. There is, indeed, nothing that can be said about the interests of the United States in an Isthmian canal that does not apply now with equal force to the Strait of Florida. The one links the Atlantic to the Gulf, as the other would the Atlantic to the Pacific. It may be added here that the phenomenon of the long, narrow peninsula of Florida, with its strait, is reproduced successively in Cuba, Haiti, and Puerto Rico, with the passages dividing them. The whole together forms one long barrier, the strategic significance of which cannot be overlooked in its effect upon the Caribbean; while the Gulf of Mexico is assigned to absolute seclusion by it, if the passages are in hostile control.

The relations of the island of Jamaica to the great barrier formed by Cuba, Haiti, and

[1] There is Charlotte Harbor, at 120 miles, but it can be used only by medium-sized vessels.

Puerto Rico are such as to constitute it the natural stepping-stone by which to pass from the consideration of entrance into the Caribbean, which has been engaging our attention, to that of the transit across, from entrance to the Isthmus, which we must next undertake.

In the matters of entrance to the Caribbean, and of general interior control of that sea, Jamaica has a singularly central position. It is equidistant (500 miles) from Colon, from the Yucatan Channel, and from the Mona Passage; it is even closer (450 miles) to the nearest mainland of South America at Point Gallinas, and of Central America at Cape Gracias-á-Dios; while it lies so immediately in rear of the Windward Passage that its command of the latter can scarcely be considered less than that of Santiago. The analogy of its situation, as a station for a great fleet, to that for an army covering a frontier which is passable at but a few points, will scarcely escape a military reader. A comparatively short chain of swift lookout steamers, in each direction, can give timely notice of any approach by either of the three passages named; while, if entrance be gained at any other point, the arms stretched out towards Gallinas and Gracias-á-Dios will give warning of transit before the purposes of such transit can be accomplished undisturbed.

With such advantages of situation, and with a harbor susceptible of satisfactory development as a naval station for a great fleet, Jamaica is certainly the most important single position in the Caribbean Sea. When one recalls that it passed into the hands of Great Britain, in the days of Cromwell, by accidental conquest, the expedition having been intended primarily against Santo Domingo; that in the two centuries and a half which have since intervened it has played no part adequate to its advantages, such as now looms before it; that, by all the probabilities, it should have been reconquered and retained by Spain in the war of the American Revolution; and when, again, it is recalled that a like accident and a like subsequent uncertainty attended the conquest and retention of the decisive Mediterranean positions of Gibraltar and Malta, one marvels whether incidents so widely separated in time and place, all tending towards one end — the maritime predominance of Great Britain — can be accidents, or are simply the exhibition of a Personal Will, acting through all time, with purpose deliberate and consecutive, to ends not yet discerned.

Nevertheless, when compared to Cuba, Jamaica cannot be considered the preponderant position of the Caribbean. The military question of position is quantitative as well as qualitative; and situation, however excellent, can rarely, by itself alone, make full amends for defect in the power and resources which are the natural property of size — of mass. Gibraltar, the synonym of intrinsic strength, is an illustration in point; its smallness, its isolation, and its barrenness of resource constitute limits to its offensive power, and even to its impregnability, which are well understood by military men. Jamaica, by its situation, flanks the route from Cuba to the Isthmus, as indeed it does all routes from the Atlantic and the Gulf to that point; but, as a military entity, it is completely overshadowed by the larger island, which it so conspicuously confronts. If, as has just been said, it by situation intercepts the access of Cuba to the Isthmus, it is itself cut off by its huge neighbor from secure communication with the North American Continent, now as always the chief natural source of supplies for the West Indies, which do not produce the great staples of life. With the United States friendly or neutral, in a case of war, there can be no comparison between the advantages of Cuba, conferred by its situation and its size, and those of Jamaica, which, by these qualities of its rival, is effectually cut off from that source of supplies. Nor is the disadvantage of Jamaica less marked with reference to communication with other quarters than the United States — with Halifax, with Bermuda, with Europe. Its distance from these points, and from Santa Lucia, where the resources of Europe may be said to focus for it, makes its situation one of extreme isolation ; a condition emphasized by the fact that both Bermuda and Santa Lucia are themselves dependent upon outside sources for anything they may send to Jamaica. At all these points, coal, the great factor of modern naval war, must be stored and the supply maintained. They do not produce it. The mere size of Cuba, the amount of population which it has, or ought to have, the number of its seaports, the extent of the industries possible to it, tend naturally to an accumulation of resources such as great mercantile communities always entail. These, combined with its nearness to the United States, and its other advantages of situation, make Cuba a position that can have no military rival among the islands of the world, except Ireland. With a friendly United States, isolation is impossible to Cuba.

The aim of any discussion such as this should be to narrow down, by a gradual elimination, the various factors to be considered, in order that the decisive ones, remaining, may become conspicuously visible. The trees being thus thinned out, the features of the strategic landscape can appear. The primary processes in the present case have been carried out before seeking the attention of the reader, to whom the first approximations have been presented under three heads. First, the two decisive centres, the mouth of the Mississippi and the Isthmus. Second, the four principal routes, connecting these two points with others, have been specified ; these routes being, 1, between the Isthmus and the Mississippi themselves ; 2, from the Isthmus to the North American coast, by the Windward Passage ; 3, from the